# How to Write a Kindle Ebook

A step-by-step guide

DAVID P MITCHELL

Copyright © 2020 David P Mitchell

All rights reserved.

ISBN-13: 979-8-66-287128-1

# DEDICATION

To Andrew, Gráinne, Mairéad, Róisin & Cormac

# CONTENTS

|   | Preface | i |
|---|---|---|
| 1 | What Should I Write? | 1 |
| 2 | Front Matter | 6 |
| 3 | Basic Formatting | 12 |
| 4 | Footnotes/Endnotes | 16 |
| 5 | Images | 22 |
| 6 | Table of Contents | 32 |
| 7 | The Book's Cover | 38 |
| 8 | Converting Your Word File to HTML | 46 |
| 9 | Uploading Your Book to KDP | 50 |
| 10 | Making Changes After Publication | 68 |
| 11 | Promoting Your Book | 72 |
| 12 | Looking Ahead | 79 |
|   | Appendix: KDP Select | 80 |

# PREFACE

Writing your first ebook might seem daunting, much like any other technical task you've never attempted before. In fact, it's something anyone with basic computer skills can do – you just have to know how.

I wrote my first ebook, Skiing Made Easy, in 2018. I found the information I needed by reading Building Your Book for Kindle, looking at the Help pages on the Kindle Direct Publishing ('KDP') website, and studying some topics in more depth.

I spent quite a lot of time on research, and ended up with a good understanding of the subject. This book is the result of that research: it's designed to draw together the knowledge I gained, and present it as a single, complete resource. I believe it will save you a lot of time when working on your own ebook.

The less time you have to spend on the technical aspects of publishing an ebook, the more you can devote to what really matters – the story you want to tell.

## What does this book cover?

There are lots of ways to write an ebook, and I don't cover all of them.

I assume that you, like me, just want to find one good way to write and publish your book; a way of writing and publishing it that is straightforward, but produces a professional-looking and profitable product.

I used Microsoft Word to write Skiing Made Easy, and I published it as a Kindle ebook. That's the method I describe here.

### Why write an ebook?

The traditional publishing process involves finding an agent to represent you; the agent in turn finds a publisher for your work. The costs of publishing physical books are high, so publishers want to be pretty certain that they are picking winners. Only a lucky few are accepted by an agent and a publisher – many of them famous already.

If you have an idea that you want to turn into a book, and you're not, say, Oprah Winfrey or Donald Trump, it might be hard to publish it in the traditional way. If you decide to write it as an ebook, nobody can stop you. The only upfront cost is the time you put into it.

### Why Kindle?

Amazon's Kindle was the first e-reader, launched in 2007; Kindle owners could go to the Kindle store and buy Kindle ebooks to read on their devices. These days, you don't have to have a Kindle device to read Kindle ebooks – you can simply download a Kindle app to your phone, tablet, Mac or PC.

Ebook sales are growing[1]. Although it now has competitors, Kindle still dominates the ebook market. 2017 figures show that it had an 83% market share in the US, and 88% in the UK[2]. Apple's iBooks came a distant second, at 9% (US) and 7.5% (UK).

You might argue that it's not healthy for a market to be so dominated by a single business, and in the long run that dominance could reduce the bargaining power of authors and ebook buyers. That's true. Still, Kindle's market share is a persuasive argument for starting there.

Once you've written and published your Kindle ebook, that could be the time to investigate the other options – iBooks, Barnes & Noble, Kobo, Google Play, and more.

### Why Microsoft Word?

I used Microsoft Word quite simply because that's what KDP recommends. I found that it worked perfectly well, so now I recommend it too.

### The structure of this book

This book is designed to help you write your own ebook.

It begins with a chapter called 'What Should I Write?' Even if you already know what you want to write about, Chapter 1 will help you tailor your subject to the ebook format.

The chapters that follow cover all the practical steps needed to publish your book. There's advice on formatting, footnotes, images, creating a cover, uploading your book to KDP, promoting and advertising it, and more.

## An image gallery

This book contains images, to illustrate the steps I describe with real examples.

When printing a book, colour is much more expensive than black and white. To keep costs down and make sure the price of the book is reasonable, it's printed in black and white. You can find the images in colour on my website at https://howtowriteanebook.info/image-gallery/.

## British spellings

Except when quoting, I use British spellings. If you're reading this in the US and see the word 'colour' or 'centre', you might think I've been drinking too much 'whisky' – but that's how those words are spelt in the UK.

I hope any American readers will forgive what may seem to you to be unusual orthography!

# 1 WHAT SHOULD I WRITE?

The chances are, you already know what you want to write about. Still, it's worth looking at the types of ebook people buy. Even if this chapter doesn't influence your first project, it might spark ideas for subsequent books.

There are other related considerations, too. How long should your book be? Is it worth producing a series of books?

## The most popular categories of ebook

Amazon doesn't make much sales information available, so it's not straightforward to find out the most popular categories of ebook. You have to adopt the methods of Sherlock Holmes: collect evidence, piece it together, and reach a logical conclusion.

That's what Publishing With Love did in late 2019[3].

They looked at the first, fiftieth and one hundredth (#1, #50, & #100) best-selling books in each Amazon category, and noted the ranking of those titles relative to the whole store. Using this information they were able to produce a table showing the popularity of each ebook category.

The author of the article says that book #100 in any category is a good indicator of the niche in general.

### Fiction

In their 'fiction' table, the top category based on the #100 title was Literature & Fiction; that was followed by Romance, then Mystery, Thriller & Suspense. (Those were the rankings when I looked in March 2020; the tables are updated from time to time).

### Non-fiction

Geoff Affleck did something similar in 2017, looking specifically at non-fiction. He published an article entitled '10 Best Selling Non-fiction Book Topics'[4].

For the purposes of his piece, Affleck looked at ten non-fiction categories on Amazon.com, and noted the Amazon Bestseller Rankings of the top five books in each one. This enabled him to calculate an average ranking for each category.

These were the top non-fiction ebook categories (with the average ranking of the top five books in that category in brackets):

1. Religion & Spirituality (#61)
2. Biography & Memoir (#96)
3. Business & Money (#123)
4. Self-help (#146)
5. Cook books, Food & Wine (#171)

Affleck notes that the most popular ebooks were fiction, accounting for 94 of the top 100 books in the Kindle store at the time of his research – so only 6 were non-fiction. In print, 64 of the top 100 were fiction, and 36 were non-fiction. He concludes that most of us prefer our non-fiction books in print.

But Affleck adds, 'If you're writing a non-fiction eBook, don't be discouraged – the market is huge for non-fiction eBooks that are well-written and solve specific problems for their readers.'

### My own research

I did a little research of my own in March 2020.

When I first navigated to the Kindle Books section of Amazon.co.uk, I was presented with 'Top Picks for You', and the Top Pick for Me was 'How to Win Friends and Influence People', by Dale Carnegie.

For all their tracking and technology, Amazon doesn't always know its customers very well. Hell would have to freeze over before I bought a book like that. Not that I'm criticising the book – I'm sure it's very good, and I definitely wish I was on the receiving end of the Royalties from it. It's just not my kind of title…even if plenty of people would say it's exactly what I need to read!

Heaven only knows what the Top Pick for Me will be now that I've clicked on so many books that don't interest me for my research. Anyway, what did I find out?

Although Amazon doesn't publish sales figures, it does have a page showing 'Best Sellers in the Kindle Store'. It's updated hourly, so it's a snapshot of popular ebooks at a particular moment. This is what I noticed on Amazon.co.uk on 3rd March 2020:

- The top three books were all thrillers/murder mysteries
- The top ten books were all fiction
- The first non-fiction book (at #11 in the chart) was a memoir
- The top book which was neither fiction nor memoir (#28) was 'The Courage to be Disliked' by Ichiro Kishimi. It is in the self-help category, but I feel it might amount to self-hindrance for me, and I would do better to avoid it
- There were no 'how to' guides in the top 100

I also used 'the Geoff Affleck method' to find the most popular non-fiction categories on Amazon.co.uk.

The results should be treated with caution, because categorising books is an art not a science, and many books appear in more than one category. For example, a novel about a girl who wanted to marry a fireman and open a bakery popped up in the 'food & drink' category, but it was in others too.

The top five non-fiction categories (with the average ranking of the top five books in that category in brackets) were:

1. History (#47) - a category dominated by Hilary Mantel
2. Politics & social science (#81). The big caveat here is that the top sellers were not genuinely politics or social science books; for example, one was a novel about a retired army sergeant called Boonzie McCulloch
3. Self-help (#82)
4. Biography & true accounts (#117)
5. Parenting & families (#142) - but the top sellers were actually novels, not parenting manuals

## Summary on the most popular categories of ebook

It is useful to know the most popular categories of ebook. If your main goal is to make as much money as possible, then write a thriller or a romance – or do something that's more reliably profitable than writing a book. Otherwise, I suggest just doing the best job you can on the topic you want to tackle. That will be satisfying in its own way.

## Length of an ebook

When checking out ebooks on a particular topic, I came across a work that attracted some negative comment. One review of it was titled 'What? Two pages!!! I want my money back.' The text of the review began: 'This is not a book.' Another reviewer's considered opinion of the same work was 'absolute rubbish.'

That book was too short, but how long should your ebook be?

Opinions vary.

### Make a Living Writing blog

There is, or was, a theory that ebooks should be shorter than traditional print books. 'People don't tend to read for hours on end on a digital screen, and they tend to go for shorter ebooks for that reason.'[5]

That quote is from Carol Tice on the Make a Living Writing blog, in an article written in 2012. She believes ebooks should be shorter, but not everyone agrees.

### Smashwords

The founder of Smashwords, Mark Coker, argues that the shorter ebook theory isn't really true[6]. His analysis of ebook sales on Smashwords '...indicates a strong preference among customers for longer ebooks.'

Coker says that Smashwords' top 10 best selling titles average 121,000 words. As word count decreases, sales decrease. However, on the day (in 2012) when he wrote the article, the average word count of ebooks published on Smashwords was just 37,000.

How many words per page? That's fluid on Kindles, because readers can choose their own font size, and the number of pages changes accordingly. As a general rule, though, Amazon says a page is 300-350 words[7]. (Images increase the length of a book).

That means that Smashwords' best-sellers are around 372 pages long, but the average title published there is 114 pages.

### Book Cave

According to Catia Shattuck of Book Cave[7], works of fiction tend to be longer than non-fiction books, but non-fiction books are generally more expensive. 'This is because they require more research and fact-checking and can become valuable resources to readers.'

The average fiction ebook is 246-307 pages (80,000-100,000 words); the average non-fiction ebook is 153-230 pages (50-75,000 words). 10,000 words of solid content should be the minimum for a non-fiction ebook, says Shattuck.

This book is around 18,000 words, because that's how many I needed! It has a lot of images, and Amazon's product details for the ebook version say that it is 146 pages.

### A series of books

So there's no hard-and-fast rule that ebooks should be shorter. Still, I believe there's merit in the advice Carol Tice gives in the Make a Living Writing blog post I mentioned, which is titled '10 Mistakes I Made Publishing My Ebook'.

Instead of publishing one long book in three parts, she says she would have been better advised to release three short books. Then she could have started earning sooner, and she would have had more than just a one-off product.

Joanna Penn makes a similar point about writing a series of books[8]. '[H]aving multiple books in a series is the best way to gain reader loyalty and sales for the long term,' she writes. She adds, 'If you're an ebook reader, you'll know how powerful a series can be.' When a reader finishes one book in the series, they're notified about the others, which helps sales.

### Summary on length of an ebook

These, then, are the main points about the length of an ebook:

- Don't make your work really short just because it's an ebook. Best-selling fiction is around 372 pages or 121,000 words
- A non-fiction book can be shorter - 153-230 pages or 50-75,000 words
- 10,000 words of solid content should be regarded as the minimum for a non-fiction book – otherwise your reviewers might say 'this is not a book!'
- It's worth considering splitting a long work into two or more shorter ebooks
- A series of books can help you make a living

## 2 FRONT MATTER

The structure of your ebook will be front cover, front matter, main content in chapters, then endnotes.

The front cover is the image that appears in the Kindle Store, and it plays a key role in selling your book. However, it is separate from the book itself – it doesn't form part of the Word file that contains your book.

For that reason, the front cover is often the last thing authors create, and I'll leave it to the end.

The first part of your Word file will be the front matter of your book.

There's information on 'Building the Front Matter of Your Book' in Amazon's Building Your Book for Kindle pdf⁹, which dates from 2012. (It's also available as a free ebook in the Kindle Store). KDP Help has more up-to-date guidance.

The front matter of the book includes:

- Title page
- Copyright page
- Dedication
- Preface or Prologue

KDP says that as a minimum there should be a title page; the other front matter pages are optional, but desirable.

### Title page

First, open a new document in Microsoft Word with File > New Blank Document. (There may be slight differences between versions of Word; mine is Word 2011 for Mac).

In the new document click on the 'centre-aligned text' icon in Word's

Home tab, and type the title of your book, then your name underneath. Then enter a page break (Insert > Break > Page Break).

Imagine my book title is 'The Tiger, the Wizard & the Chest of Drawers'. This is what my title page will look like.

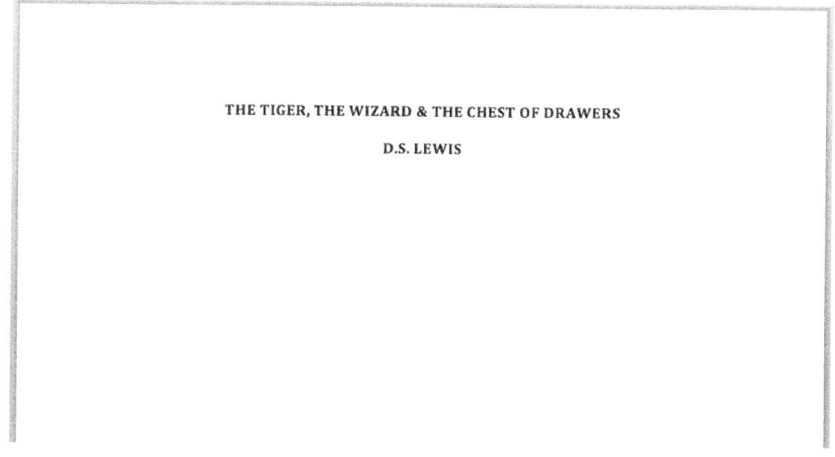

Figure 1: title page

Remember, you can see colour versions of the images on my website at https://howtowriteanebook.info/image-gallery/.

### Save your document

This is a good time to save the new document (File > Save As > [enter name you choose for your document in the dialog box that opens] > Save). I've called my document tiger-wizard-chest.docx. (Docx is the default Word file format from 2007 onwards – before that, it was .doc).

### Create an images folder

If your book is going to have pictures in it, I suggest creating an 'images' folder in the directory where you saved your Word document. Then all your images are in one place and it's easy to keep track of them.

### Back up

It's a good idea to back up your document (and images folder) now, and keep doing it every time you add to it or change it. If you've spent hours writing your book and put your heart and soul into it, you'll be devastated if you lose it all because of an IT malfunction.

If you save the primary copy of your document to the 'Documents' directory of your computer, you could use an external hard drive for the backup copy. I would avoid using a USB memory stick, because in my experience they sometimes stop working suddenly.

### Check the line and page breaks with the 'pilcrow' option

A helpful feature of Word allows you to see the line and page breaks you've inserted.

In the menu at the top of the Word document window is a funny backwards 'P' symbol, known as a pilcrow. The pilcrow was '…used in the Middle Ages to mark a new train of thought, before the convention of visually discrete paragraphs was commonplace.'[10] It's now used on Word (and other word processing software) to show breaks.

If you click on the pilcrow option in Word, pilcrow symbols will appear where you've put in line breaks; and where you inserted a page break, there'll be a pilcrow and the words 'Page Break'.

This is what it looks like.

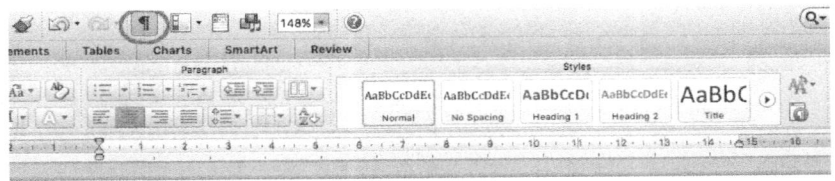

Figure 2: pilcrow option activated

I can then toggle the pilcrow option off again if I wish.

### Copyright page

After the page break, create a copyright page.

Like the title page, the text should be centred. Building Your Book for Kindle suggests this wording: 'Text copyright © 2012 John Q Smith', then underneath 'All rights Reserved'.

On my Mac, I use the option key (in between ctrl and cmd) + g to type the copyright symbol. On Windows, it is ctrl + alt +c.

Since I have images in my books, I've modified the suggested wording slightly. It looks like this.

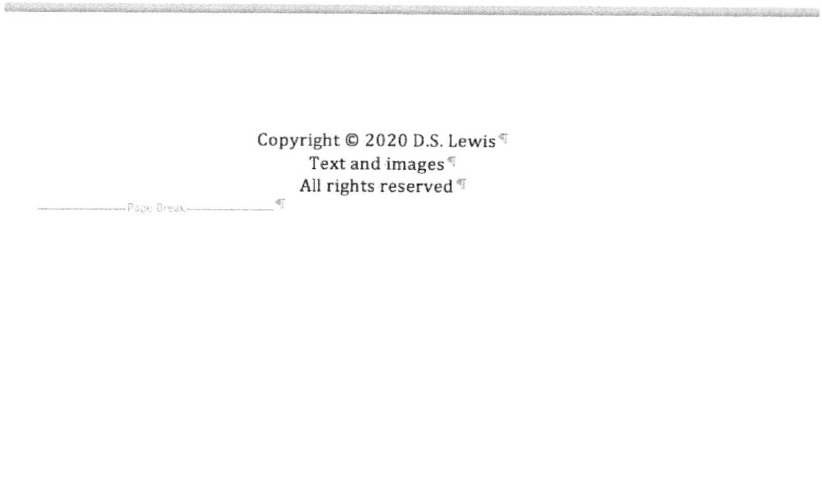
Copyright © 2020 D.S. Lewis¶
Text and images¶
All rights reserved¶
-----Page Break-----¶

Figure 3: copyright page

Insert another page break after the copyright information.

## Dedication

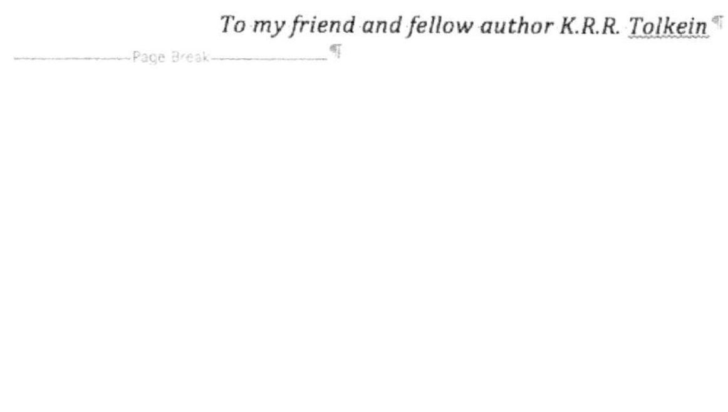
*To my friend and fellow author K.R.R. Tolkein*¶
-----Page Break-----¶

Figure 4: dedication page

You don't have to dedicate the book to anyone, but it's a nice idea. Like the other front matter pages, it should have centred text, and be followed by a page break.

I've used bold for the title page and italics for the dedication. Bold and italics will transfer across to Kindle format. (On the other hand, because font and font size can be selected by the reader on a Kindle device or app, the author of the book can't specify them).

## Table of contents

What comes next?

Building Your Book for Kindle is ambiguous on this point. It says the Preface and/or Prologue should follow the dedication page, but it also says that the Preface/Prologue should come after the Table of Contents.

It makes sense to put the Table of Contents before the Preface/Prologue.

For the moment, I'll simply type 'Table of Contents' on a page as a placeholder. (Before typing, I click on the 'left-aligned' icon in Word's Home tab, so my Table of Contents isn't centre-aligned).

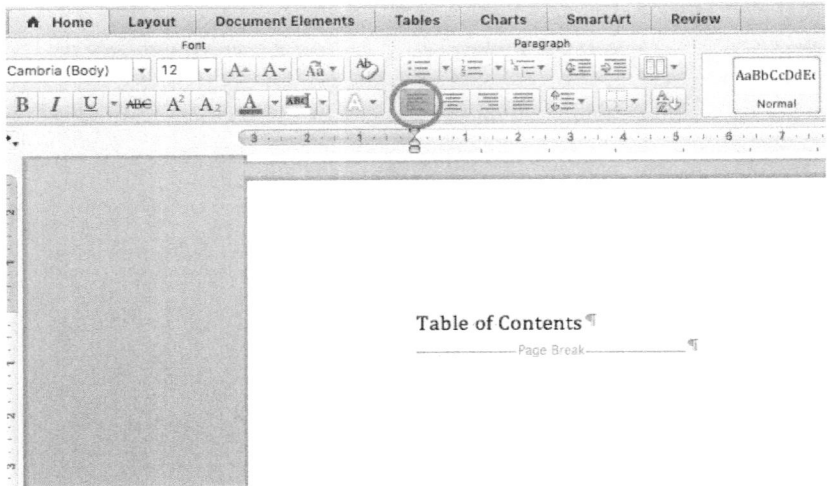

Figure 5: Table of Contents placeholder

I won't create the full Table of Contents now, though. It will be easier to do it once I've written my book, when all the chapter headings are in place. That's why I cover the Table of Contents in Chapter Six.

## Preface/Prologue

The last item of front matter is the Preface or Prologue (or both).

What is a Preface? It's an introduction to the book written by the book's author (as opposed to a foreword, which is written by someone else). A Preface explains how the idea for the book was developed, and can include acknowledgements to other people who helped the author during the time of writing[11].

What is a Prologue? A work of fiction can have a Prologue, containing '…an important element of the story that took place prior to the book's main plotline'[12].

Since this is a non-fiction book, I've included a Preface. It explains how I came to write the book, what it covers, and why it may help readers. It also contains the web address of the website that accompanies the book.

The Tiger, the Wizard & the Chest of Drawers is a (fictional) work of fiction. It could have a Preface and a Prologue, but as an example I've written a short Prologue to it. It tells the story of the making of the chest of drawers, many years before the events in the main chapters of the book.

> **Prologue**
> Many years ago, so long ago that nobody alive today can say precisely when, an aged carpenter stood in his workshop, looking at a chest of drawers.
>
> The carpenter's apprentice entered by the back door. 'Is it finished, Master?' he asked. 'It is solid and beautiful. Surely it will sell for a handsome price!'
>
> 'I believe it may indeed be my finest work,' replied the carpenter. 'But it is not for sale. This chest is destined for the lonely house on the edge of Beech Forest. There it will stay for two hundred years, until a curious child finds it and uses it as the door to a secret world.'
>
> The apprentice looked on in wonder, as the carpenter's eyes sparkled.
>
> --------- Page Break ---------

Figure 6: Prologue

The formatting of the Prologue is the same as that of the main chapters. As I've now covered all the elements of front matter, I'll move on and deal with formatting, in Chapter 3, Basic Formatting.

# 3 BASIC FORMATTING

Your book has to be formatted in a particular way to ensure that it still looks right after it has been converted to Kindle format.

## Chapter headings

Continuing with the example of The Tiger, the Wizard & the Chest of Drawers, I'll type 'Chapter One', then a couple of paragraphs of text. Before formatting, it looks like this.

> Chapter One
> Paul, Sandra, Edward and Lisa have been evacuated from London during World War II, and sent to live in the English countryside by Beech Wood.
> Lisa finds a solid and beautiful chest, and clambers into one of the drawers. Suddenly she finds herself in a secret world, the land of Nurnia.
> In Nurnia, Lisa meets a roe deer.
> ——Page Break——

*Figure 7: chapter heading & text without formatting*

Now I need to turn 'Chapter One' into a Word 'Heading 1'. I highlight 'Chapter One' and under 'Styles' on Word's Home tab I click on 'Heading 1'. That's all I have to do to make it a top-level heading.

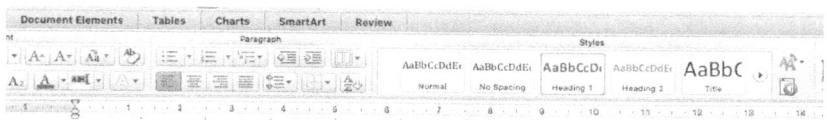

Figure 8: chapter heading as Word Heading 1

The default format of a Heading 1 will do for now. If I want to change it, I can right-click on the Heading 1 button, select 'Modify', then choose my styling.

If you've already styled your chapter headings, you can right-click on the Heading 1 button, and select 'Update Heading 1 to match selection'. Your styling will become the new default for all top-level headings.

Making the chapter heading a 'Heading 1' is recommended because it will support easy navigation within your book for the reader.

## First line indents & spacing after

Next, I'll set first line indents for the paragraphs, and create space after each paragraph.

To do this, I click Format > Paragraph, and a dialog box opens. In the dialog box, I select:

- Indentation > Special: First Line > By 1.27cm
- Spacing > After > 12pt

Then I click OK to apply the changes I've specified. The first line of the paragraph will be indented, and there'll be space after the paragraph.

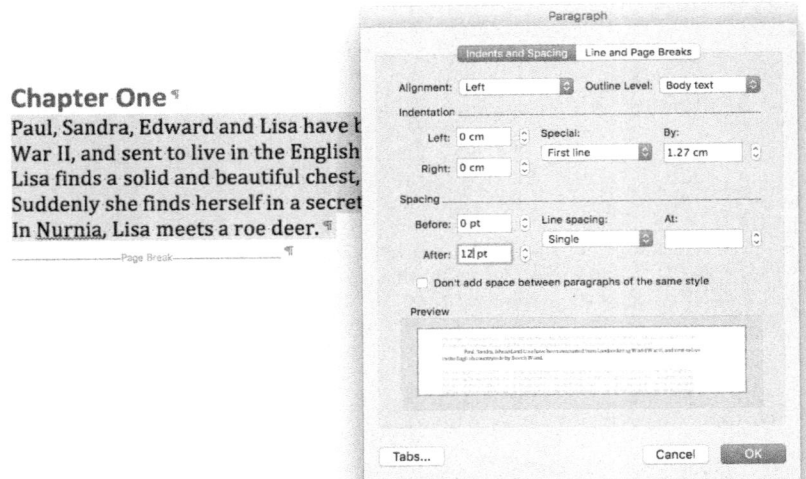

Figure 9: indent and spacing after paragraph

You don't have to choose 1.27cm and 12pt. Building Your Book for Kindle suggests 0.5" and 10pt.

It is important, though, to use the method I've outlined. Don't be tempted to create indentation by hitting the tab key, and space between paragraphs by tapping away at Enter/Return – your formatting won't translate to Kindle.

When I next press Enter to start a new paragraph, my formatting is retained: I automatically get the same first line indentation and space after.

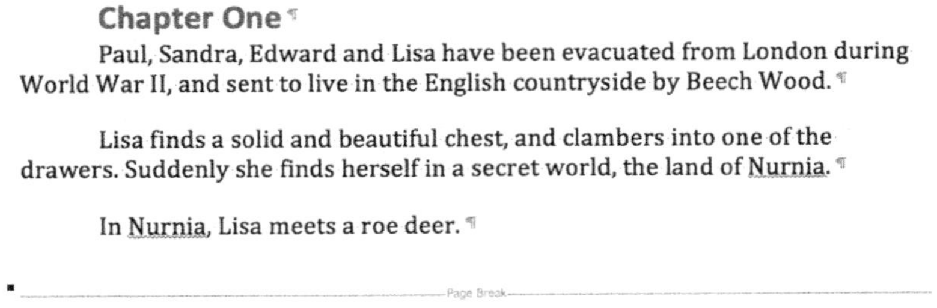

Figure 10: formatted text

To my eye, the placement of 'Chapter One' would look odd unless flush with the first line, so I've indented it.

## Sub-headings

You're more likely to use sub-headings in a non-fiction book like this one, than in a work of fiction.

When writing a web page, I would always follow a logical order of headings, using h1 for the main page heading, h2 for the next level, and so on. It's good practice to do the same when writing your Kindle ebook.

A chapter should have just one 'Heading 1' (the chapter heading); the next level of sub-heading is 'Heading 2', and there can be several such sub-headings, of equal importance; below a 'Heading 2' there can be one or more 'Heading 3's.

Word offers 'Heading 4', 'Heading 5' and 'Heading 6' too.

## Headers and footers

Building Your Book for Kindle advises: 'Headers, such as title and chapter, and footers, such as page number, will not display on Kindle as intended; avoid using them.'

## The next chapter

When I've finished a chapter, I insert a page break, and apply the same basic formatting to the next chapter.

I'm going to insert a page break now, and begin my next chapter, which is about footnotes and endnotes.

# 4 FOOTNOTES/ENDNOTES

If you're writing a non-fiction book, you may wish to put references in footnotes or endnotes.

You can't use footnotes at the bottom of each page, because a Kindle book is fluid rather than having set pages. Instead, you have to use endnotes – references that appear at the end of the book.

This works well when reading on Kindle, because if you click or tap on a reference number in the text, the footnote appears as a pop-up at the bottom of your screen. The pop-up footer gives you the option to 'Go To Footnotes', but mostly you won't need to.

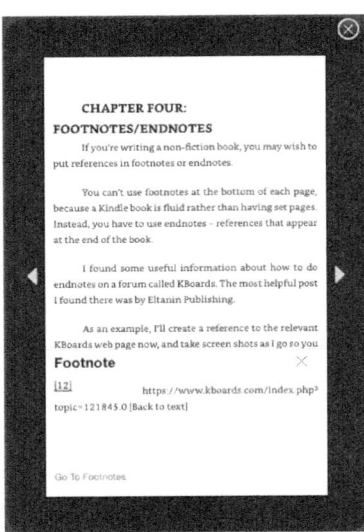

Figure 11: pop-up Footnote on Kindle Previewer

I found some useful information about how to do endnotes on a forum called KBoards. The most helpful post there was by Eltanin Publishing.

As an example, I'll go through the process of creating an endnote (in the ebook version of this book) with a reference to the relevant KBoards web page. I'll include screen shots so you can see all the steps.

The reference to KBoards is here[13].

1) To insert the endnote into the manuscript of my ebook, I place my cursor where I want the reference to go, and from the menu bar at the top of my screen I choose Insert > Footnote, and select Endnotes. (I keep the default continuous numbering, so Word will count my endnotes for me; this one is number 12 in the ebook).

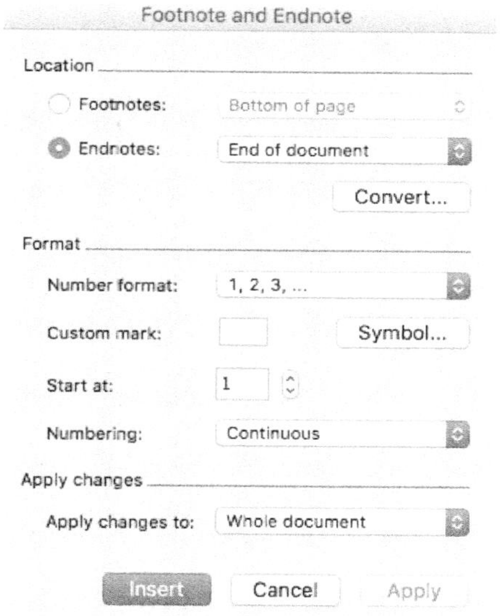

Figure 12: inserting an endnote

As soon as I click the 'Insert' button, Word adds the number of the endnote to my text in superscript, and it automatically scrolls to the end of my document, where it has already inserted the endnote number.

2) I can now add the web address I want to reference, as the endnote. I copy it from my web browser's address bar, and paste it next to the endnote number.

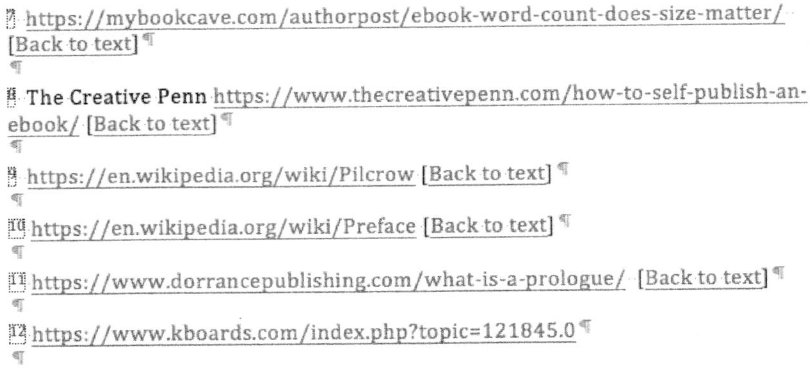

[7] https://mybookcave.com/authorpost/ebook-word-count-does-size-matter/ [Back to text]

[8] **The Creative Penn** https://www.thecreativepenn.com/how-to-self-publish-an-ebook/ [Back to text]

[9] https://en.wikipedia.org/wiki/Pilcrow [Back to text]

[10] https://en.wikipedia.org/wiki/Preface [Back to text]

[11] https://www.dorrancepublishing.com/what-is-a-prologue/ [Back to text]

[12] https://www.kboards.com/index.php?topic=121845.0

Figure 13: KBoards web page added as endnote 12

3) Next, I insert a bookmark by endnote 12. I use Insert > Bookmark, and in the dialog box that opens, I choose a name for the bookmark and click 'Add'. I'm using a consistent naming system for my endnote bookmarks, and this one is called 'footnote12'.

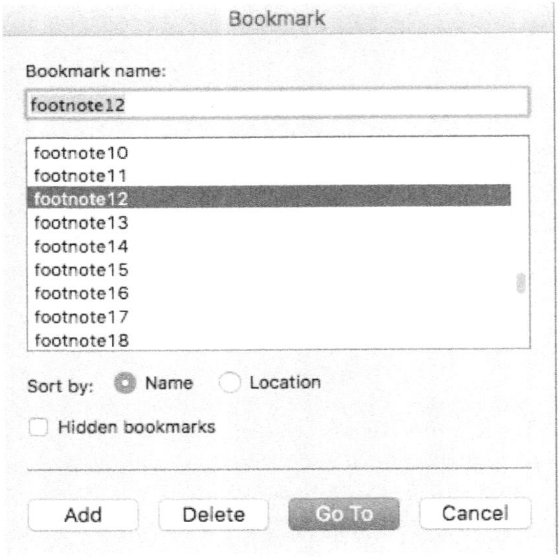

Figure 14: inserting a bookmark by the endnote

4) Now I'll go back to Chapter 4, highlight the '12' that Word inserted in my text, and insert a link from it to the endnote bookmark I've just created.

I select Insert > Hyperlink, and a dialog box opens. I choose to link to my 'Document' (not a 'Web Page'). Then where it says 'Anchor', I click on

'Locate'. This opens a new dialog box, where I can click to expand the Bookmarks, and select 'footnote12'.

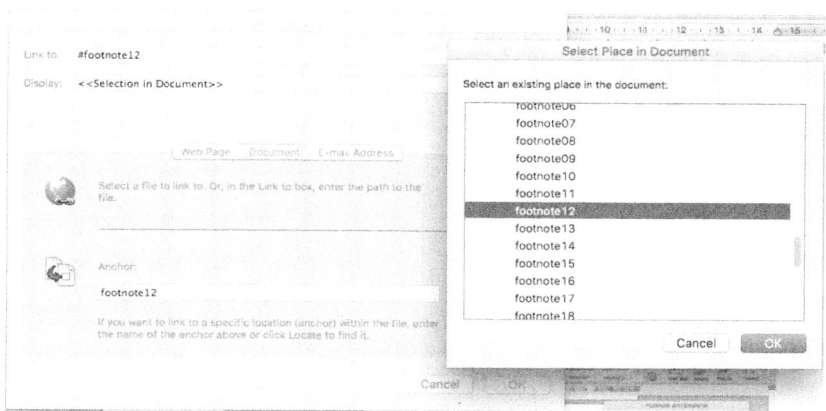

Figure 15: inserting a link to an endnote (footnote12)

5) Next, I need to insert a bookmark at the start of the paragraph that contains a reference to endnote 12. I'll use Insert > Bookmark, and call the bookmark 'back12'.

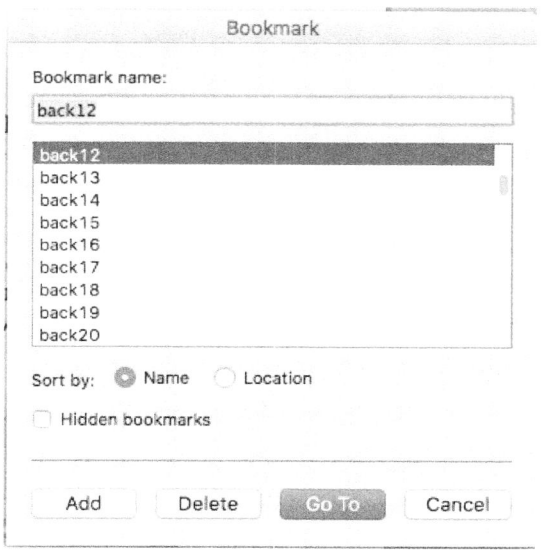

Figure 16: inserting a bookmark at reference 12

I should now be able to follow the link from my reference 12 to the endnote. (For some reason if I just click on '12' it doesn't work, but I can right-click on it and choose Hyperlink > Open Hyperlink; that takes me to the endnote).

6) The last step is to create a link from the endnote back to the bookmark I've just inserted in Chapter 4. Then, if a reader follows the link to the endnote, they can easily get back to where they were in the text.

Immediately after endnote12, I'll type '[Back to text]'. To link it to the bookmark 'back12', I use Insert > Hyperlink, and as before I choose 'Document', 'Locate', and find the bookmark in the second dialog box that opens.

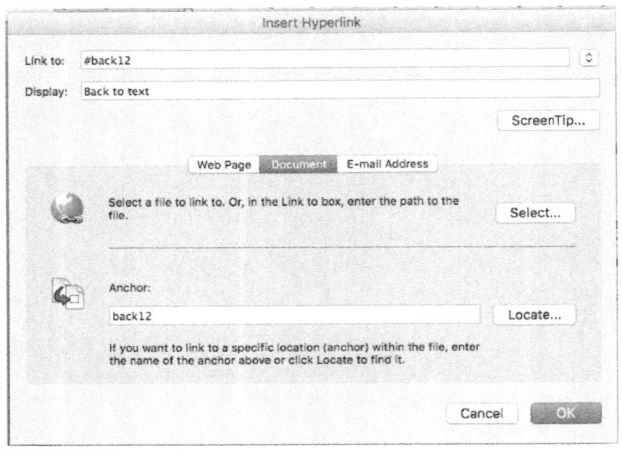

Figure 17: linking back to reference 12

Now if I click on 'Back to text', it takes me to the Chapter 4 paragraph containing reference 12.

To summarise, the steps are:

1. Insert an endnote using Insert > Footnote, and choose 'Endnote'
2. Add a web page reference and/or other text where the endnote appears at the end of your document
3. Insert a bookmark by the endnote, using Insert > Bookmark, and choose a name for the bookmark according to a consistent system
4. Create a hyperlink from the endnote reference number in your text to the endnote itself
5. Insert a bookmark at the start of the paragraph that contains the endnote reference number, again using a consistent naming system
6. Go to the endnote, and create a hyperlink from there back to the bookmark inserted in step 5

That should do it. You now have a reference that links to the relevant endnote, and a [Back to text] link to return to your place in the book.

Word doesn't usually display bookmarks, but I can make it reveal them by selecting Word > Preferences > View, and ticking the box by (Show) Bookmarks.

Then I can see all the bookmarks I've inserted. They a look a bit like bookends. These are the bookmarks I've inserted by my endnotes.

⚑⁴ https://geoffaffleck.com/10-best-selling-non-fiction-book-topics/ [Back to text]

⚑⁵ https://www.makealivingwriting.com/excuse-earning-freelance-writer-now/ [Back to text]

⚑⁶ https://www.huffpost.com/entry/do-ebook-customers-prefer_b_1457011 [Back to text]

⚑⁷ https://mybookcave.com/authorpost/ebook-word-count-does-size-matter/ [Back to text]

⚑⁸ https://www.thecreativepenn.com/how-to-self-publish-an-ebook/ [Back to text]

⚑⁹ https://en.wikipedia.org/wiki/Pilcrow [Back to text]

⚑¹⁰ https://en.wikipedia.org/wiki/Preface [Back to text]

⚑¹¹ https://www.dorrancepublishing.com/what-is-a-prologue/ [Back to text]

⚑¹² https://www.kboards.com/index.php?topic=121845.0 [Back to text]

Figure 18: bookmarks inserted by endnotes

As I don't find the bookmark symbols distracting, and it is useful to see where they are, I'll keep the setting that makes them display.

I've used quite a lot of screenshot images in this chapter, to illustrate the steps to take when creating endnotes. Clearly then, you can include images in Kindle ebooks, but it isn't totally straightforward. Whatever steps you take, KDP will degrade the quality of your images and there's nothing you can do about it.

Images are covered in the next chapter.

# 5 IMAGES

Building Your Book for Kindle has just two short paragraphs about images, which might lead you to believe that there's not much to know about them. If you did think that, you'd be mistaken.

I'll cover the topic in depth, but first let's look at the advice in Building Your Book.

### What Building Your Book for Kindle says about images

Building Your Book's first paragraph on images recommends using JPEGs, and explains how to insert them.

It's worth following the recommendation to use JPEGs (.jpg or .jpeg file extension). If you use a different file format, your images will be turned into JPEGs anyway when your book is converted to Kindle format[14].

The images should be centre-aligned, and inserted using Insert > Picture/Photo (not copy and paste).

### Inserting an image

As an example I'll insert an image into The Tiger, the Wizard & the Chest of Drawers.

When I press Enter to start a new paragraph, Word keeps the first line indentation I've been using (1.27cm). In fact, I don't want my image to be indented. I could just press backspace/delete to get to the margin, but that wouldn't that translate to consistent formatting on Kindle.

I have to use Format > Paragraph, and set the indentation to '(none)' in the dialog box that opens.

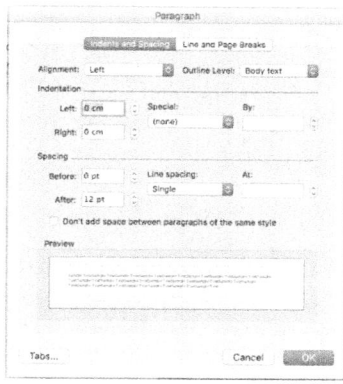

Figure 19: setting indentation to none

Now on the Home tab I click on the 'centre-aligned text' icon, and from the menu bar at the top of the screen I choose Insert > Photo, and select 'Picture from file...'. In my case, I then wait a few seconds for a dialog box to open.

As I suggested in Chapter 2, on my computer I have a folder that contains:

- The Word document where I'm writing my book, and
- A sub-folder called 'images' with the images for the book

That way, all the images are in one place, and it's easy to find the one I want to insert.

In the dialog box, I navigate to my 'images' folder, choose an image and click 'Insert'. This is the result.

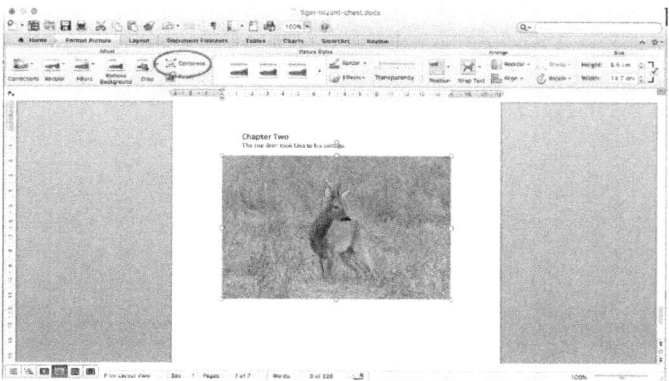

Figure 20: image inserted

Word is keen to compress images, but I'd rather it didn't. After inserting the image, I can click 'Compress' (circled in Figure 20), and a dialog box opens. The default option is 'Best for printing (220ppi)', but instead I choose 'Keep current resolution' and 'Apply to: All pictures in this file'. Then it should hold good for other images I insert.

On Windows, default compression can be turned off by selecting File > Options > Advanced > Image Size and Quality > [select your document name] > Do not compress images in file.

### Adding a caption

There isn't any advice about captions for the images in Building Your Book[15]. I would like my caption to be 'glued' to the image – so that the caption and image never appear on different pages of the resulting ebook. As far as I know, that's not possible.

Instead, I use Word's captions. Although such captions can be separated from the images they describe in the Kindle book, at least they have distinctive styling which makes their purpose clear. Also, the numbering is automatic; and if I go back and insert an image and caption earlier in my document, all the later image captions are re-numbered without me having to do anything.

With the image still selected, I choose Insert > Caption… and in the dialog box that opens, I add a description of the image.

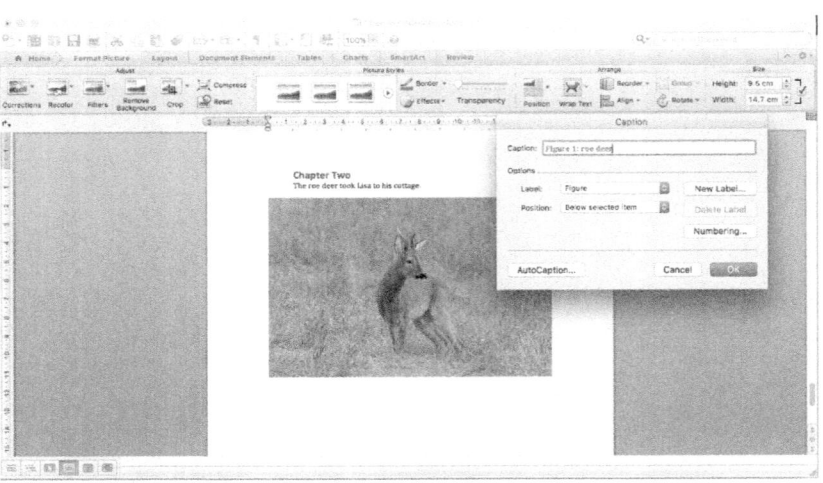

Figure 21: image caption

Those are the basics of inserting an image and a caption.

## Greyscale images in Kindle e-ink devices

Building Your Book's second paragraph about images says that Kindle e-ink devices don't display them in colour, but in sixteen shades of grey. Kindle Fire devices, and Kindle apps for PC, Mac etc, do show images in colour.

There's nothing you can do about that – except include a link to your images somewhere else. I'll suggest a way of doing that in a moment.

But that's not all there is to know about images.

## Other Kindle image issues

There are two related issues to consider with Kindle images. They are:

- Image quality, and
- Delivery Costs

## Image quality

William Spaniel sums up some of the frustrations with images for Kindle[16]. 'This process is going to suck...[Y]ou will become unbelievably frustrated at some point. Accept it now...'

What are the frustrations? One of them is that the Kindle conversion process mangles your images, so they don't look very good in the finished ebook.

William Spaniel again: 'Kindles (and the .mobi file extension) were created to display text. Images were very clearly an afterthought. However pretty your image looks on your computer screen, it is not going to look nearly as pretty once you have uploaded it. Sorry.'

That's a shame, and it would be a big backwards step if we couldn't have pictures in our ebooks. After all, '[b]ook illustration has existed in some form since the advent of the written word' (Literary Hub[17]). Monks and nuns created illustrated manuscripts from the sixth century onwards[18]. In Europe from the fifteenth century, text and images were carved into the same wooden block, to make block-books.

You'd think in the 2020s, we'd have the technology for picture books!

One specific image quality issue Spaniel identifies is that Kindle '...eliminates random lines of pixels from your images.' This can be especially problematic if an image contains words in a font where some parts of the letters are very narrow.

You can't write a useful 'learn to ski' book without a lot of images, and Skiing Made Easy has ninety-two.

In my experience, Spaniel is correct: the quality of the photos in the Skiing Made Easy Kindle ebook is just about adequate, but readers may suspect that some of them were taken with a potato not a camera.

### Delivery Costs

Related to the issue of image quality is that of 'Delivery Costs'. This is money Amazon charges you depending on the overall file size of your book – and images contribute a large proportion of file size.

Derek Murphy points out the problem[19]: if you choose 70% Royalties, Amazon reduces the amount you earn by charging Delivery Costs of $0.15 per 1MB book file size in the US, or £0.10 in the UK.

The alternative to 70% Royalties is 35%, in which case Delivery Costs don't apply. The problem - and you might be ahead of me here - is that 35% is quite a lot less than 70%.

This is the relevant part of Amazon's Digital Pricing Page, with the 35% Royalties option in the left hand column, and the 70% option on the right.

Not applicable - we don't deduct Delivery Costs when calculating your Royalties.

Delivery Costs are equal to the number of megabytes we determine your Digital Book file contains, multiplied by the Delivery Cost rate listed below.
- Amazon.com: US $0.15/MB
- Amazon.ca: CAD $0.15/MB
- Amazon.com.br: R$0.30/MB
- Amazon.co.uk: UK £0.10/MB
- Amazon.de: €0,12/MB
- Amazon.fr: €0,12/MB
- Amazon.es: €0,12/MB
- Amazon.in: INR ₹7/MB
- Amazon.it: €0,12/MB
- Amazon.nl: €0,12/MB
- Amazon.co.jp: ¥1/MB
- Amazon.com.mx: MXN $1/MB
- Amazon.com.au: AUD $0.15/MB

Figure 22: Delivery Costs

Derek Haines mentions[20] that only Amazon charges for ebook sales delivery. 'Other ebook retailers manage to deliver without any additional charges at all.'

You might think you can just check the size of your Word file before you upload it to Kindle, to see what Delivery Costs you'll be charged. In fact, that won't tell you much. The Word file for this book is just under 10MB and it converts to a Kindle file of less than 2MB.

John Doppler confirms that 'what you put in isn't what you get out' (Self-publishing Advice[21]). For example, a .mobi file (which is the basis of the older Kindle file formats), contains multiple versions of the ebook. The file size will be three to four times larger than that of the finished Kindle, so isn't a good guide to Delivery Costs. The Kindle conversion process '…eliminates many of the differences between formats.'

How can you find out your exact file size? When you upload your book file to KDP (see Chapter 9), the dashboard will tell you the file size and Delivery Costs (Figure 23). This is the place to find the definitive answer.

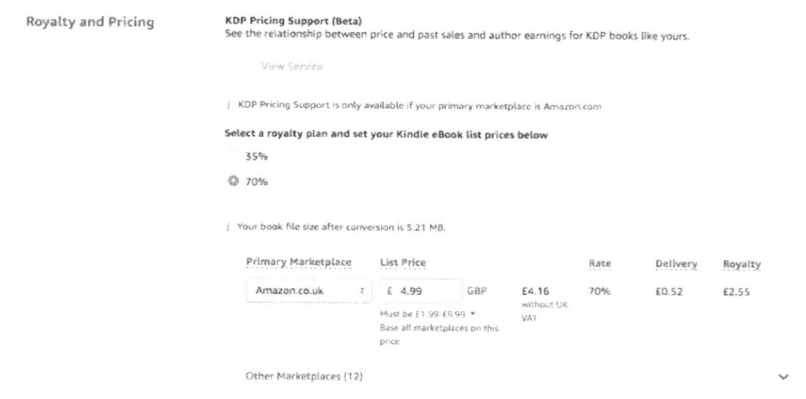

Figure 23: KDP Pricing & Delivery Costs for Skiing Made Easy

The published book's file size is displayed on Amazon in the 'product details'.

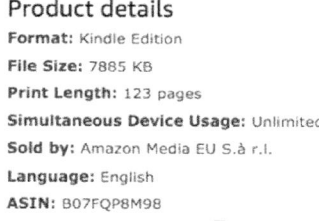

Figure 24: Skiing Made Easy product details

In the case of Skiing Made Easy, this information doesn't match that on the KDP dashboard. I'm charged for 5.21MB (52p), but the Amazon product details give a file size of 7.88MB. Therefore, the product details are not a reliable guide to file size for the purposes of Delivery Costs.

Out of interest, if I look at the actual size of Skiing Made Easy as downloaded to my computer to read on my Kindle app, it's 8.1MB. The downloaded files look like this.

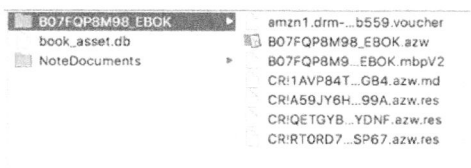

Figure 25: Kindle ebook files

I believe the different component files are as follows:

- The .voucher file is connected to Digital Rights Management (preventing the free transfer of the book to other devices or formats)
- The .azw file is the text of the book itself
- The .mbpV2 file allows me to annotate my copy of the book
- The azw.md file contains Mark Down, or formatting information
- The azw.res files contain images; it could be that there are three different versions of the images, at different resolutions

Again, the actual size of the files appears to be greater than the file size Amazon charges me for. For once, this is a discrepancy to my advantage!

Anyway, the lesson is that the *only* place you get an accurate Delivery Cost is on the KDP upload dashboard.

### Calculating Delivery Costs

Incidentally, I don't actually lose 52p per sale of Skiing Made Easy. The Delivery Cost is taken off before my 70% royalty is calculated, so I lose 70% of 52p, which is 36p.

The calculation is based on my sale price of £4.99 including VAT (sales tax). The price of the book is £4.16 without VAT.

£4.16 - £0.52 Delivery Cost = £3.64 x 70% royalty = £2.55

So I get £2.55 per sale, whereas without Delivery Costs I would get £2.91.

### Front cover

Your front cover, which is displayed in the Kindle store, is usually uploaded separately from the book itself. John Doppler thinks that it doesn't affect file size and Delivery Costs, but it could if you embed a copy of the cover in your book file.

### Solutions to Kindle image issues

What can authors do about the twin issues of image quality and delivery costs?

### Image quality

The pictures in a learn to ski book are very important, and I haven't found a way of placing top-quality images in the Kindle ebook itself. That's why I decided to create a Skiing Made Easy image gallery on my website, and include a link to it near the start of the book.

The images from Skiing Made Easy are in a photo gallery on my ski website[22]. As you know, I've made a similar photo gallery for the images that go with this book[23].

To create these photo galleries, I installed WordPress on my websites, and used WordPress's image gallery in combination with a plugin called Simple Lightbox. That generates a gallery and slideshow.

There are other ways to make a photo gallery. If you don't have a website, you could open an account on Flickr.com, and put the images in an album. Flickr will create a slideshow.

### Delivery Costs

How can you retain a reasonable image quality within your Kindle book, but reduce Delivery Costs as much as possible? Darcy Pattison has some valuable ideas[24].

Pattison looked at the KindleGen software that actually turns other files into Kindle format, and at the images it produces.

She found that KindleGen created a Scaled-Images folder, with images 1000px wide. She believes these are the images actually delivered to readers, even if the images submitted to KDP by the author are larger. Her conclusion is that there's no point in submitting bigger images, because they may increase your file size and Delivery Costs but they won't translate into better images for the reader.

Pattison also discusses the quality at which you save your images, as this has a big impact on file size. When you've finished editing an image in Photoshop or similar photo-editing software, you can save it as a JPEG and specify the quality.

JPEG is a format which allows image compression – so that the file size is reduced. It is called 'lossy' compression: some image information is discarded, on the basis that the human eye often can't tell the difference anyway, to achieve a small file size.

If you push it too far and lose too much image information, then people will be able to see that the image is poor quality.

Pattison says that a quality of 40, on a scale of 0-100, is good enough and results in a small file size.

### Compressing an image in Photoshop

My photo-editing software is Photoshop Elements 15. I start with the highest-quality version of the image I have – usually a Raw image if it's a photo I've taken with my camera. The reason for starting with a high-quality image is that if you compress an image that has already been compressed, you start to multiply the loss of quality.

After any editing and cropping, I can 'Save for Web'. Here's an example of a photo from Skiing Made Easy.

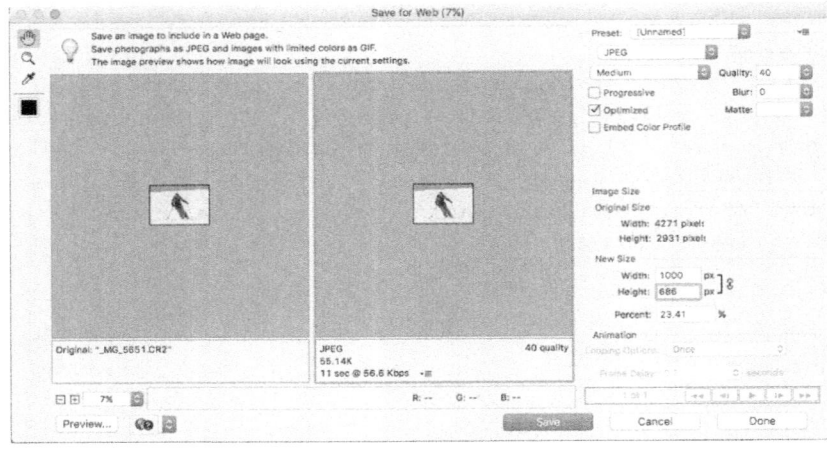

Figure 26: saving a photo as a JPEG

Following Darcy Pattison's recommendation, I save it at 1000px wide and a quality of 40.

If we compare file sizes at different stages, they are:

- 35.8MB for the original Raw image
- 6.1MB for the JPEG at full pixel width (4271) and 100 Quality
- 402.1KB for the JPEG at 1000px width and 100 Quality
- 55.1KB for the JPEG at 1000px width and 40 Quality

That leaves me with a fairly modest file size.

If you don't have Photoshop or equivalent software, you could use a free online photo-editing tool such as https://ipiccy.com.

Pattison also suggests stripping EXIF data out of the image file. This is metadata - information about the camera and the image. For example, it contains the camera's Body Serial Number, and the focal length and aperture used when taking the shot.

When using 'Save for Web' on Photoshop Elements, the EXIF data is automatically removed. Another option suggested by Pattison for removing EXIF data is ImagOptim, which is available as a free download.

A remaining question

I found Darcy Pattison's article really helpful, but I still have an unanswered question.

In the Kindle conversion process, when creating the Scaled-Images folder, does KindleGen effectively process and compress already-compressed images? Would it be better to upload higher quality images, which would then be compressed by KindleGen with a better result? And would I only be charged for the Scaled-Images?

I'd like to try uploading a manuscript with high-resolution images, and the same manuscript with compressed images, to compare the result. I suspect that both may result in the same Kindle file size and the same Delivery Costs.

## Summary on images

These are the main points about images for Kindle:

- Use Insert > Picture/Photo, not copy and paste
- Centre-align the images
- You can use Word's captions for your images
- The images won't look very good in the resulting Kindle ebook
- If they are important, it is worth presenting them on your website or Flickr account, and including a link to them in the book
- Beware of Delivery Costs; images can expand your input file size dramatically
- One author advises keeping Delivery Costs down by saving images at 1000px wide and a quality of 40

Most of the images in this book are screenshots, and the file size was never huge. I didn't reduce the image quality at all before uploading the ebook manuscript to Kindle.

The images in the finished ebook don't look great, but I can't take the credit for that! KDP degraded the image quality without any assistance from me.

Originally there were a lot of whole-screen images, but in the ebook the text on those screenshots was too small and poor quality to be legible; to try to improve the reader experience, I've changed many of the images to include just the most relevant small part of the screen.

# 6 TABLE OF CONTENTS

Building Your Book for Kindle explains that Kindle readers rely on a working Table of Contents, to jump to places in the book by clicking on links embedded in the text. As there are no page numbers in Kindle ebooks, the links are to chapters and other key locations, not specific pages.

There are two ways of creating a Table of Contents – the way Building Your Book tells you to do it, and the way I prefer.

## Building Your Book's way of creating a Table of Contents

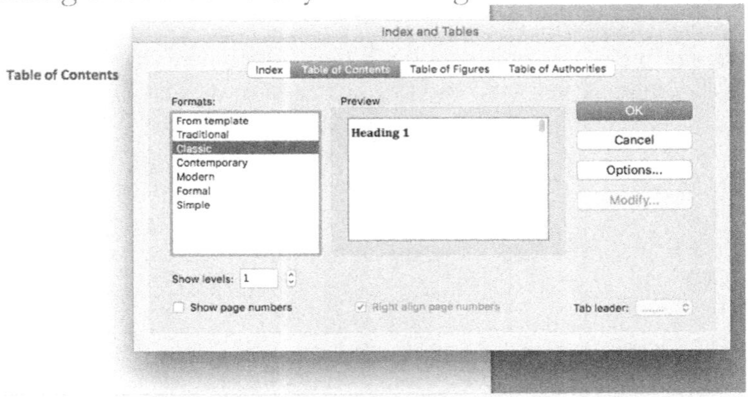

Figure 27: inserting a Word Table of Contents

Building Your Book for Kindle says you should use Word's Table of Contents function.

I'll continue with 'The Tiger, the Wizard & the Chest of Drawers' as an example. On Word for Mac, when I select Insert > Index and Tables... a dialog box opens, and in the dialog box I choose the Table of Contents tab.

I set 'Show levels' to 1 (so only 'Heading 1's – chapter headings - are included in the Table of Contents). I untick 'Show page numbers', because they aren't relevant to Kindle ebooks.

The dialog box is shown in Figure 27.

After clicking 'OK', this is the result.

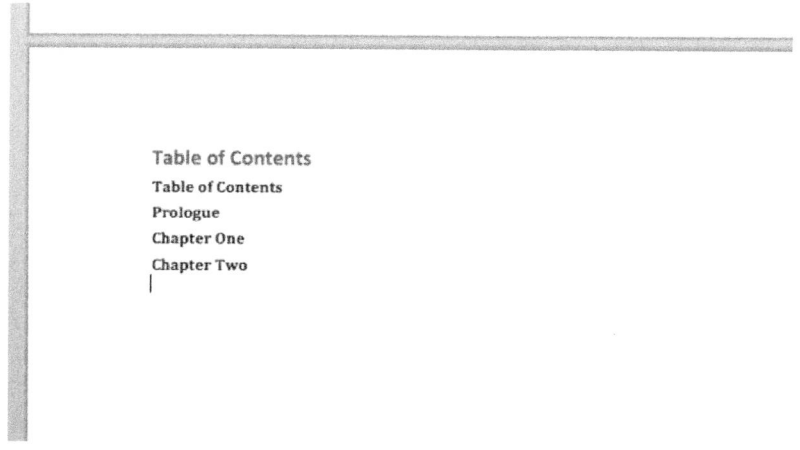

Figure 28: resulting Table of Contents

As you can see, it produces a Table of Contents. In the Word document, it's not a working Table of Contents, in that it doesn't contain hyperlinks to the chapters.

When I was writing Skiing Made Easy, I thought 'never mind, it will work once it has been converted to Kindle format'. Unfortunately, it didn't.

There's another way to insert a Word Table of Contents. Instead of using Insert > Index and Tables..., I could click on the Document Elements tab of Word's menu, then click on one of the Table of Contents icons.

That inserts a Table of Contents.

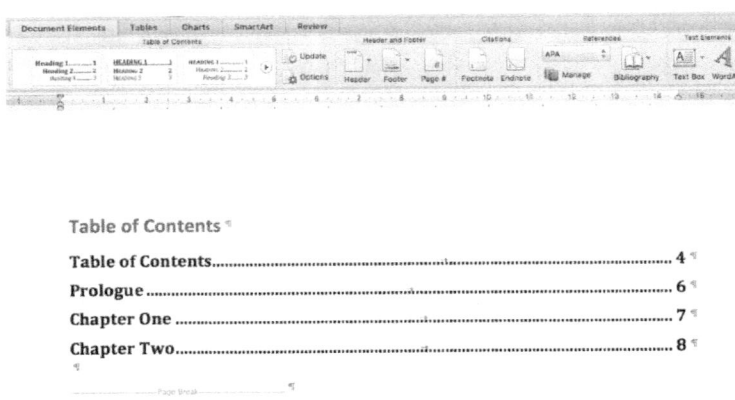

Figure 29: Table of Contents from the Document Elements tab

Then I follow the advice on KDP's Create a Table of Contents in Word Help page (more or less, because the options they suggest aren't quite what I have on my version of Word).

To the right of the Table of Contents icons on Word's Document Elements tab, I click Options, and in the dialog box that opens, I un-tick 'Show page numbers'.

After clicking OK, a pop-up box asks me, 'Do you want to replace the selected table of contents?' I click Yes, and the Table of Contents now has no page numbers.

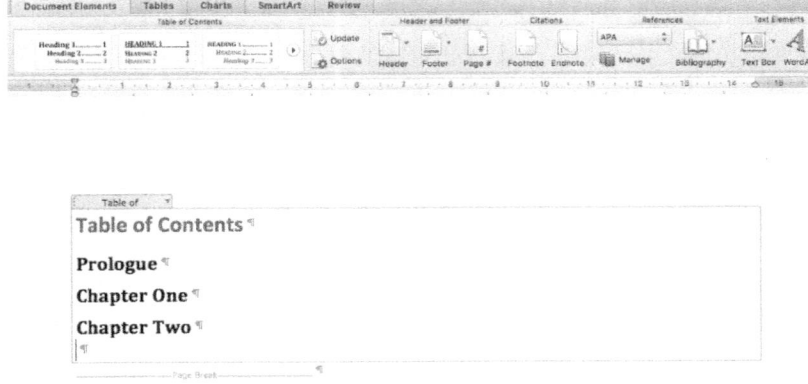

Figure 30: replaced Table of Contents

It still isn't a working Table of Contents in Word (in that it doesn't have hyperlinks). A contributor to a Microsoft Community forum[25] says that 'Word for Mac won't generate TOCs with linked titles. Only the page numbers in the TOC are linked.' If I was hoping that Word would create links to the chapter headings for me, it seems I'm going to be disappointed. If I wanted, I could create the hyperlinks manually.

Word's Table of Contents may be the right solution on Windows, but it doesn't save me any work on Mac. Instead, I prefer to create a Table of Contents manually.

## My way of creating a Table of Contents

It's no trouble to create a Table of Contents manually. The method is similar to that for endnotes (Chapter 4), but simpler because you don't need to insert bookmarks.

This time, I'll create a Table of Contents for 'How to Write a Kindle Ebook' as an example.

I type a 'Table of Contents' heading, and underneath, I add the chapter headings. Then for the first chapter heading (Preface), I highlight it and select Insert > Hyperlink. In the dialog box that opens, I make sure that 'Document' is selected, then click on 'Anchor: Locate'. This opens another dialog box.

In the second dialog box, I click to expand the Headings, and choose Preface. This screen shot shows both dialog boxes.

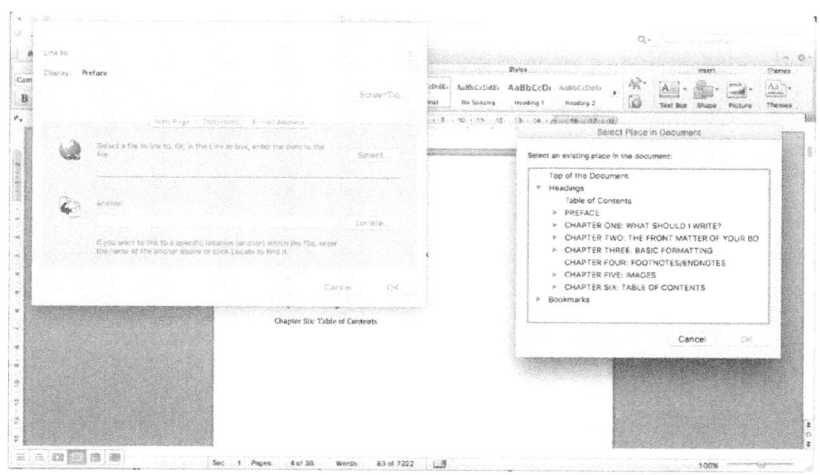

Figure 31: inserting a Table of Contents link

When I click 'OK', the link is created. Now in the Table of Contents, 'Preface' is blue and underlined, and if I click on it, it takes me to the start of the Preface. The link will also work when the book is converted to

Kindle.

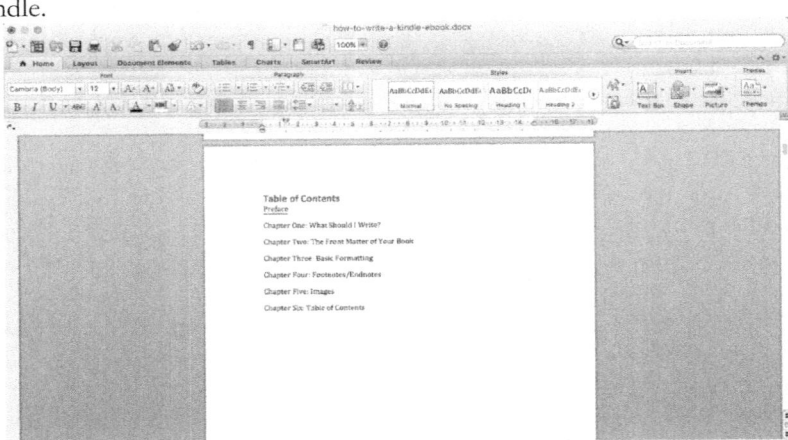

Figure 32: first link from Table of Contents completed

I can repeat these steps for the other chapters, to complete the links in my Table of Contents.

## A bookmark for the Table of Contents

Now we can return to Building Your Book's instructions. It explains that Kindle offers readers the option to 'Go To' certain places in the book, called 'Guide Items'. The Table of Contents is a Guide Item.

All that is required is to highlight the heading 'Table of Contents' and insert a bookmark called 'toc'.

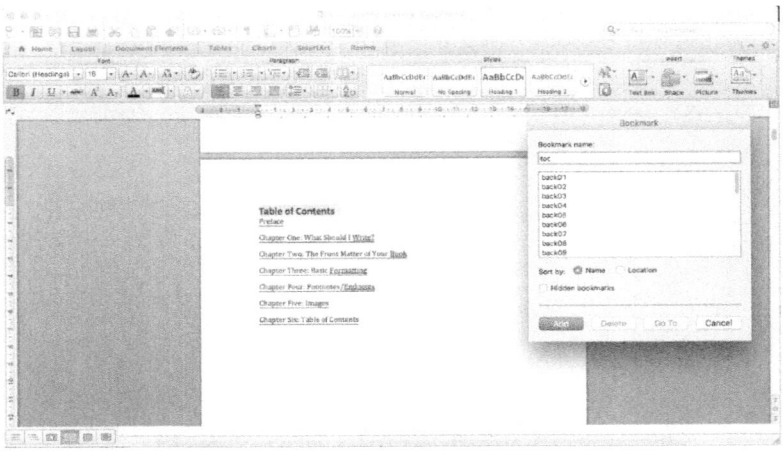

Figure 33: adding a 'toc' bookmark

If I write more chapters, I just add them to the Table of Contents in the same way. (With Building Your Book's Table of Contents method, there's a way of updating it: click anywhere in the Table of Contents, and press F9; there's also an 'Update' button in the Table of Contents section of the Document Elements tab, which performs the same function).

I've now finished work on my book's Word file. Next, I'll look at the process of creating the book's cover, before going on to examine the Kindle upload process.

# 7 THE BOOK'S COVER

Building Your Book for Kindle has just over a page of advice about the cover image for your book.
These are the main points:

- The ideal image size in pixels is 1000 (wide) x 1600 (high). This has changed to 1600 x 2560 more recently on KDP Help
- The cover should have the book title, author name, and an image which captures the essence of the book and grabs customers' attention; it should positively influences sales
- You can pay for cover design services, or do it yourself
- Make sure that your text is legible when zoomed out
- Look at top-selling books in the Kindle store to see what sells, and ask friends and colleagues for feedback
- The cover is uploaded separately from the book, and Kindle combines them in the publishing process

## Fiction book covers

I had a look at Thrillers in the Kindle store on Amazon.co.uk. Many of them include dramatic images which create an atmosphere of tension and intrigue.

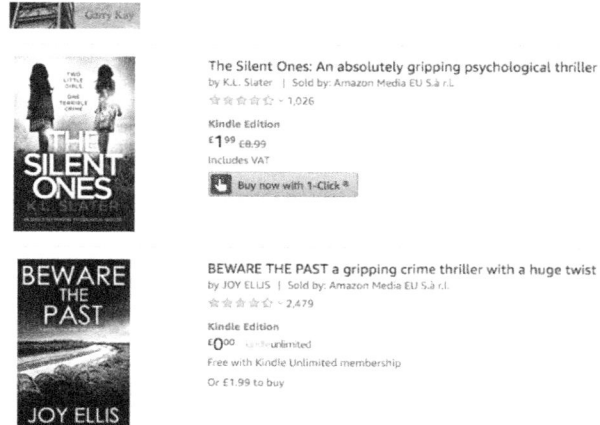

Figure 34: Thrillers in the Kindle store

Books in the Romance category feature stylised, too-good-to-be-true people on their covers.

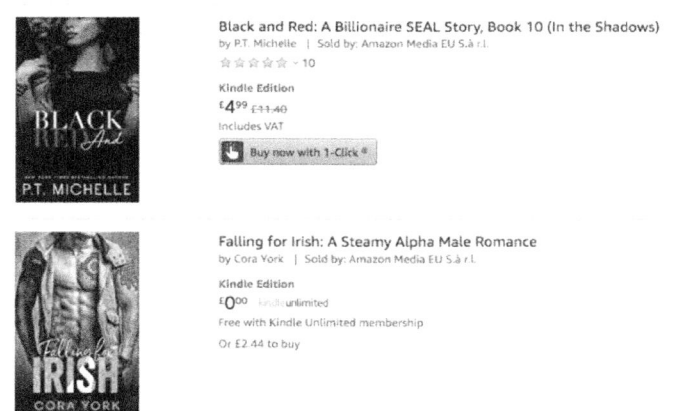

Figure 35: Romance books in the Kindle store

### 'How to write' book covers

I also typed 'how to write' into the Kindle Store search box and looked at the results it returned. These books had simple, clean cover designs.

Figure 36: 'How to write' books in the Kindle store

I rather like the cover of Anne Janzer's book. It combines the simplicity of the text box with the creativity of the 'people in the background' design.

### Three ways to create a book cover

There are three main ways to create a book cover.

The first two are DIY methods: design one with Photoshop or similar software (see below, in this chapter), or use KDP's Cover Creator (see Chapter 9).

The third possibility, if you have the budget, is to pay a professional to do it for you.

### My book's cover using Photoshop

I'm going to create a cover for this book using Photoshop Elements 15. I'm aiming for a simple, clean design – because that's what I want, not just because that's all I'm capable of!

My concept is this: a photo of a traditional book, but one that looks as though it's plugged in to an electric socket; and with a light bulb superimposed on the book to reinforce the idea that it's an electric book.

The book title and author name will be in large lettering, so they are legible even when a thumbnail image of the book is displayed in the Kindle Store.

### Create a new blank file

In Photoshop Elements, I select File > New > Blank File, and make it 1000px x 1600px, with a white background. (According to current guidelines, the size should be 1600px x 2560px). I'm calling it 'book-cover'.

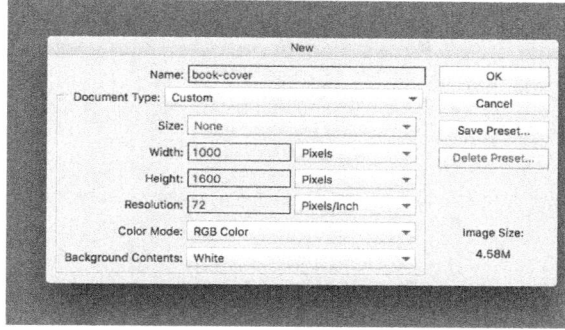

Figure 37: creating a blank file in Photoshop Elements

(The Resolution in Figure 37 is 72ppi, but KDP Help says it should be at least 300ppi).

### Add a 'book' layer

I'm using a generic hardback book, so there's no question of infringing the copyright of a cover design. I take a photo of the book, open it as a separate Photoshop file, and crop it to remove any unwanted background.

In the layers panel on the right, I have to click on the padlock symbol, so my book image becomes a layer, not a locked Background. Then I can make a duplicate layer of it, and open the duplicate layer in my 'book-cover' file.

To do this, I use Layer > Duplicate Layer… and in the dialog box that opens I name the duplicate layer 'book', make the Destination the 'book-cover' file, and click OK.

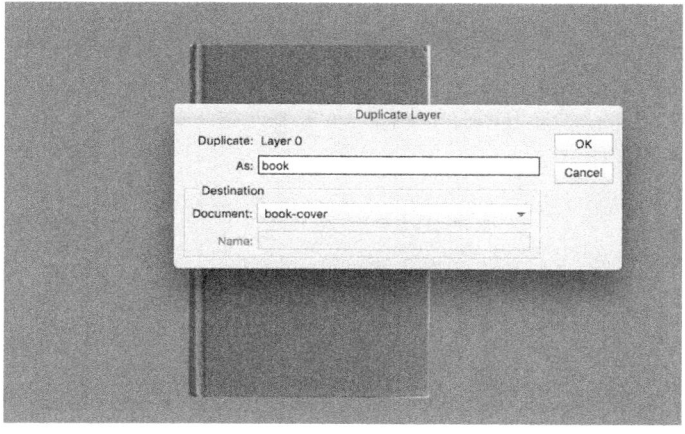

Figure 38: creating 'book' duplicate layer

(My original idea was to keep some white background, with the red book on top, but I've now decided that it will look better if the red book takes up the whole space).

After adding the 'book' layer to the Background, 'book-cover' now shows both layers in the layers panel on the right.

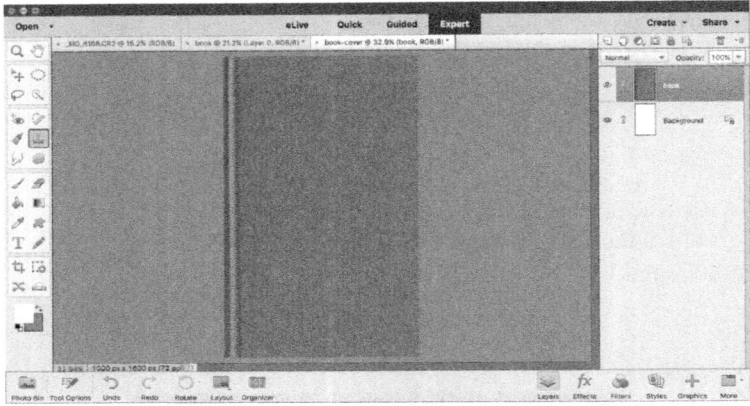

Figure 39: background and book layers

## Add a 'switch' layer

Next, I take a photo of a plug and plug socket, and open it in Photoshop. It shows as a Background in the layers panel, so I click on the padlock symbol to turn it into a layer. Then I use selection tools (the Quick Selection tool in this case) to select just the plug and socket.

Figure 40: plug and socket selected

Because I want to keep the plug and socket, and delete the background, I choose Select > Inverse – so that the background is now selected, not the plug and socket. Then I press the backspace key, and everything but the plug and socket is deleted.

I create a duplicate layer of the plug and socket and save it to my 'book-cover' file. When I look at it in 'book-cover' it's too big, but I can reduce its size:

- I make sure the plug and socket layer (which I've called 'switch') is selected in the Layers panel on the right
- In the tools panel on the left, I select the Move tool
- I go to a corner of the bounding box around the plug and socket, and push the box's handles inward to reduce the size of the image

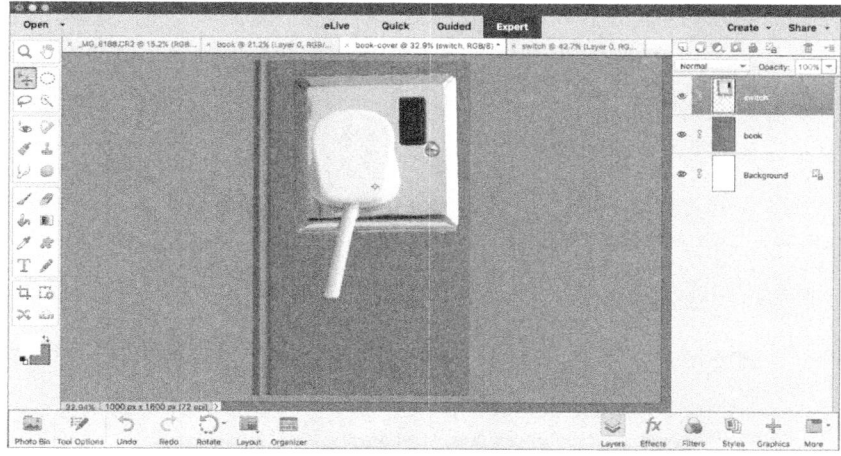

Figure 41: the 'switch' layer added to 'book-cover'

Still using the Move tool, I click and hold on the switch image, and I can move it to the top right where I want it to go.

### Add a 'bulb' layer

I've taken a picture of a light bulb, and I want that to go into the cover image too. I follow exactly the same procedure that I used for the plug and socket, to select the bulb and remove the rest of the image, and to create a 'bulb' layer in 'book-cover'. As before, I can use the Move tool to reduce the size of the bulb and position it where I want it.

This is the result.

Figure 42: bulb image added to 'book-cover'

Now all that's left to do is the text.

### Add text

I select the horizontal type tool from the tools panel on the left, and a big font size from the Tool Options at the bottom. The colour of the text will be the foreground colour I've selected on the square at the bottom of Photoshop's tools panel – in this case, white.

Figure 43: adding text to the book cover

Once I've typed my text, I can use the Move tool to make adjustments to its size and placement.

### Saving the cover image

Finally, I'll save my work.

First, I'll save the file with all the layers preserved, in Photoshop (PSD) format. That way, I can easily come back and make changes later. I use File > Save As, then choose the Photoshop/PSD file format in the dialog box that opens.

Now that the layers are safely saved, I can flatten the image to a single layer with Layer > Flatten Image, and save a copy without layers in TIFF and/or JPEG format.

I should back up the book cover image in the same place I've been backing up my book.

### Assessing the result

The cover I've produced meets the criteria I set out at the start of this chapter: the title and author name are large and legible; the pictures tell you that it's about electric books; it's not over-complicated; and the colours are bold enough to grab people's attention.

That said, it isn't going to win any awards for brilliant and innovative design, and it has a distinct homemade quality to it. Mark Twain devotees might be reminded of his Lessons in Art in Heidelberg[26].

I've continued to make changes to the cover design, and knocked it into a more or less satisfactory state.

### Professional cover design

Recently, I was looking at ebooks on a particular subject and I realised just how much influence a cover and title have on me. When looking at a page of four or five options I knew straight away which one I would pick.

Of course, before actually buying any book I read the product description, check the reviews and use Look Inside, but unless the cover and title are right I never reach that stage.

If the cover is crucial to buying decisions, it might make sense to pay a professional to do the work. It's something I'll consider for the future, and it would be interesting to see how a professional cover design affects sales in practice.

Now I've finished the book and prepared a cover, the next step is to convert my Microsoft Word file to HTML.

# 8 CONVERTING YOUR WORD FILE TO HTML

This is what Building Your Book for Kindle calls 'Finishing Your Book'.

Before you convert your document to HTML, the advice is to run a spellcheck, review your formatting, and ask a friend to proofread your manuscript.

I've nothing to add to that, except to say that any error in formatting will become obvious later – when you look at the HTML version of your work, and/or when you preview your book after conversion to Kindle. If you don't spot formatting mistakes now, you can correct them later.

## Converting your Word document to HTML

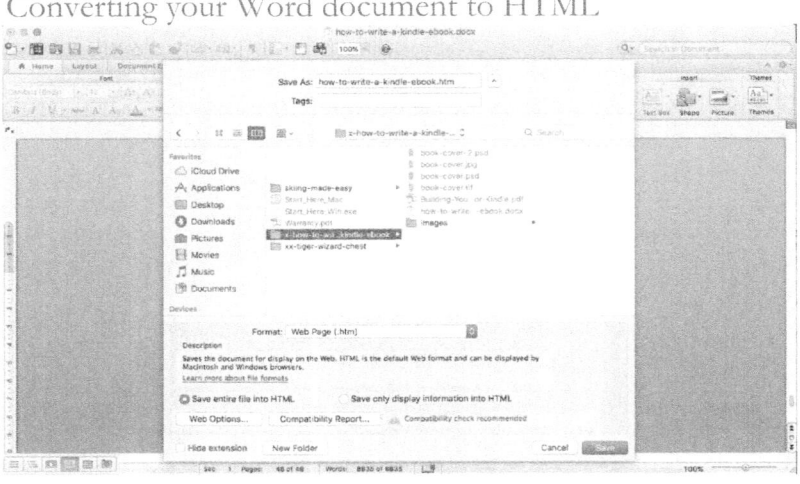

Figure 44: saving the Word document as an HTML file

Now I have to save my Word document as an HTML file.

From my Word menu, I select File > Save As, and in the dialog box that opens I choose 'Format: Web Page (.htm)' (see Figure 44 above).

(Building Your Book says the format you should choose is Web Page, Filtered (.htm, .html). That doesn't appear as an option for me, but I guess it would on a PC.)

When you click Save, the Word document disappears from your screen (although it still exists on your computer) and is replaced with an HTML document. You should find that there are no separate pages – it is one long HTML document.

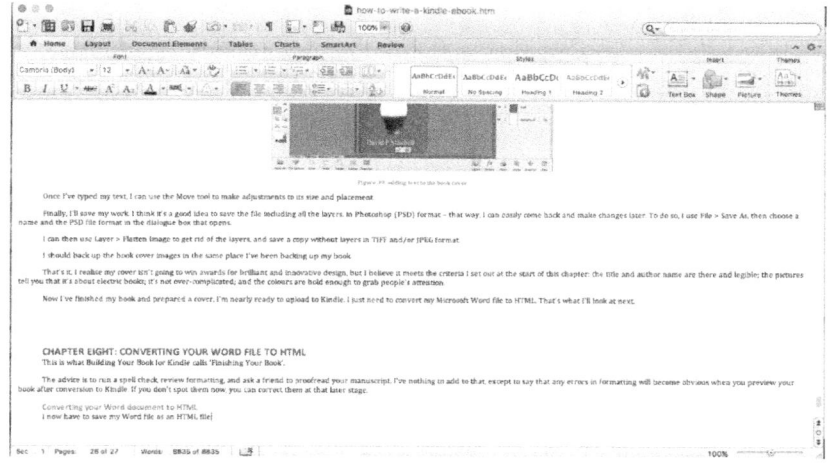

Figure 45: the HTML version of my book

You might find it interesting to read through the HTML document and, for example, check that all the images are centre-aligned. You can then close it.

If you look at the location where your files are saved, you should see that a .htm file has been created, as well as a '..._files' folder containing JPEG and GIF versions of your images (if your book has images).

I've drawn an outline around the .htm file and the '..._files' folder in Figure 46 below.

Figure 46: HTML file and new '..._files' folder

My HTML file has a Firefox icon, because that's my computer's default application for opening HTML files.

I've selected the '..._files' folder so you can see the contents.

## Zipping up the HTML file and the images

I need to create a compressed (zipped) folder containing:

- the HTML file, and
- the '..._files' folder of JPEGS and GIFS

This is how to do it.

1) Right-click and choose New > Folder. I'll call the new folder 'how-to-write-a-kindle-ebook-march-2020'.

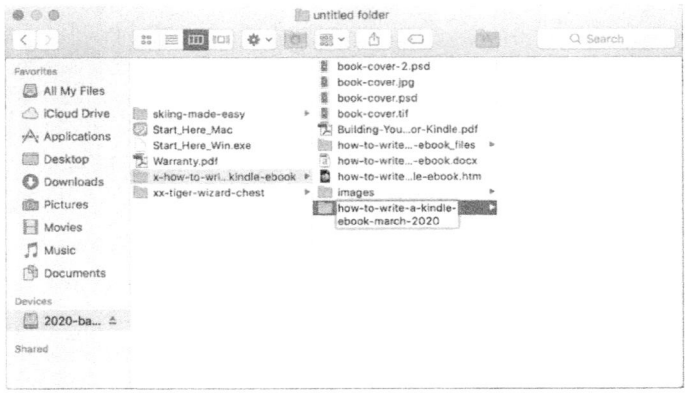

Figure 47: new folder for HTML file & images

2) Now I drag the HTML file and the '..._files' folder, and drop them into the folder I've just created.

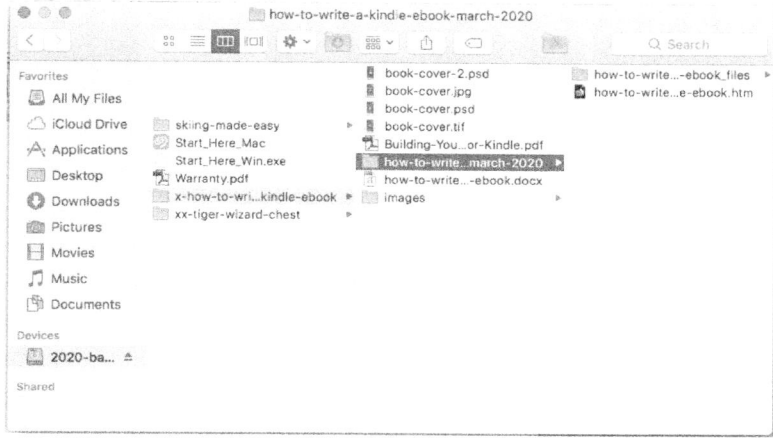

Figure 48: HTML file and '..._files' in the new folder

3) The final step is to right-click on my new folder, and choose Compress. This creates a folder called 'how-to-write-a-kindle-ebook-march-2020' with a .zip file extension.

Figure 49: zip folder

(If you don't have any images, simply compress your HTML file).

The zip folder is what I'll upload to KDP. I'm ready to start that process now.

# 9 UPLOADING YOUR BOOK TO KDP

Now to upload the book to KDP. First, I need a KDP account.

## Opening a KDP account

To create a KDP account, navigate to https://kdp.amazon.com, and you're presented with the option to Sign in with your Amazon account or Sign up (if you don't have an Amazon account).

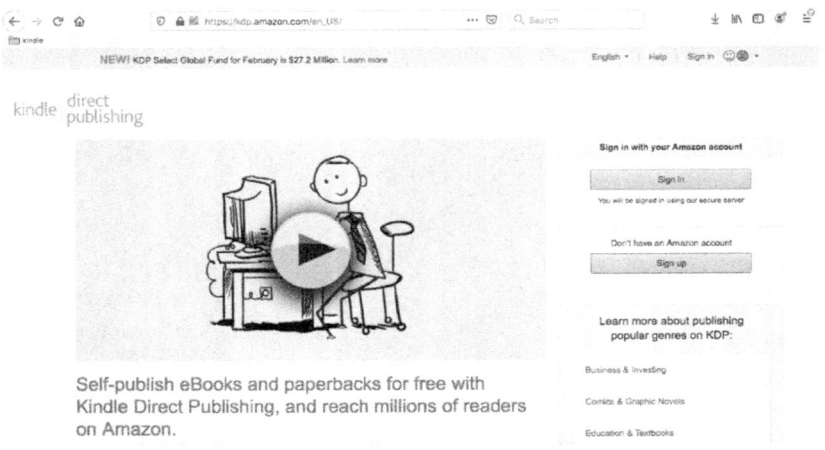

Figure 50: KDP Sign in/Sign up page

Most people have an Amazon account. In the US in 2019, there were 101 million Amazon Prime accounts – that's 62% of American households (GeekWire[27]). Most other Americans have a basic Amazon account. In the

UK, almost 90% of shoppers use Amazon[28].

Thus, nearly everyone can use 'Sign in'.

If you don't have an Amazon account and you choose 'Sign up', you're signing up for an Amazon account, not just a KDP account.

## Terms and conditions

Either way, the next step is to agree to KDP's Terms and Conditions. One of the clauses states that you're not allowed to make any public disclosures about the Terms and Conditions – so technically, I'm not allowed to tell you that I'm not allowed to tell you what's in the agreement! In reality, anyone can read the Ts and Cs, so they are not secret.

In common with all other web accounts, there's no opportunity to negotiate the terms – if you want to use the service, you agree to whatever they say. Once, you've done so, you'll be re-directed to KDP's Bookshelf page, which is in effect KDP Home.

## Account information

If you're new to KDP, you'll be greeted with the message 'Your account information is incomplete'. Click on the message, and you'll be sent to the 'My Account' page. You can also reach this part of the KDP website by clicking on 'Your Account' in the menu at the top right of the page.

There are three parts to the My Account page – Author/Publisher Information, Getting Paid, and Tax Information.

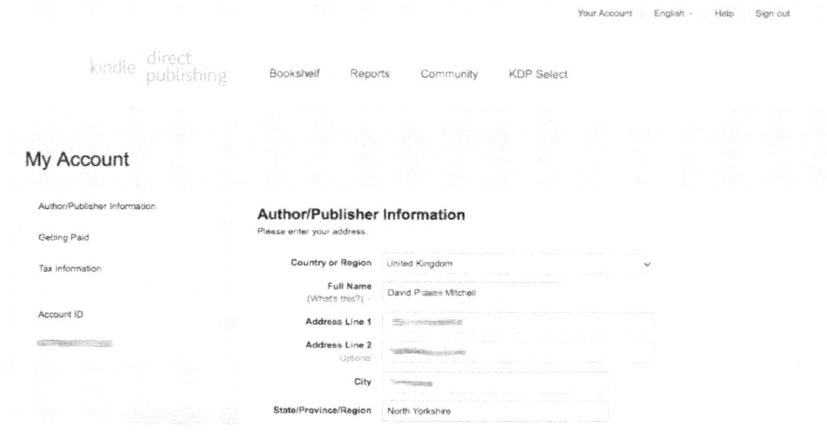

Figure 51: KDP Account Information

Provide the information requested. 'What's this?' tooltips give help for certain text boxes – just hover over 'What's this?', and extra information and tips will display.

### Author/Publisher Information

For example, you might think that 'Full Name' is self-explanatory, but the 'What's this?' advice tells you to provide the name of your publishing company or if you don't have one, your first and last name.

KDP Help topic 'Create a KDP Account'[29] stresses that you should use your real name here, not your pen name. That's because the name you enter will be used for payments and tax purposes.

### Getting Paid

Direct deposit is the preferred payment method, also known as Electronic Funds Transfer, or EFT. You get paid for a particular month's sales 60 days after the end of that month. Fair or not, that's the way it is.

The other payment options are wire transfer or cheque (check), and there are full details on KDP's Getting Paid Help page[30].

### Tax Information

You also have to provide tax information to KDP. This is done by a 'Tax Interview' which is not really an interview: it's not in person or by telephone, it's just more online form-filling.

The purpose of the Tax Interview is to comply with American tax laws. When you've completed it, an IRS W-9 form will be generated (for US publishers) or a W-8 form (for non-US publishers).

### US publishers

No part of a US publisher's Royalty payments are withheld by KDP, but the W-9 form is used to provide information to the IRS about income paid by KDP to the publisher.

### Non-US publishers

If you're a non-US publisher, KDP *could* withhold 30% of your Royalty payments for US tax. Where there's a tax treaty between the US and your country, the percentage withheld can be less, or zero. For example, if you're British and enter your UK Unique Taxpayer Reference, the withholding rate will be 0%.

IRS form W-8 is used by non-US publishers to justify exemption from US tax withholding.

Once you've completed the Tax Interview, and the information you've provided has been accepted, your Account Information page will show the message 'Tax Interview Completed:' followed by the date it was completed. Unless your circumstances change, you don't need to worry about it again.

With your account information complete, you can go to your KDP Bookshelf page.

## Uploading your book to KDP

This is the KDP Bookshelf page.

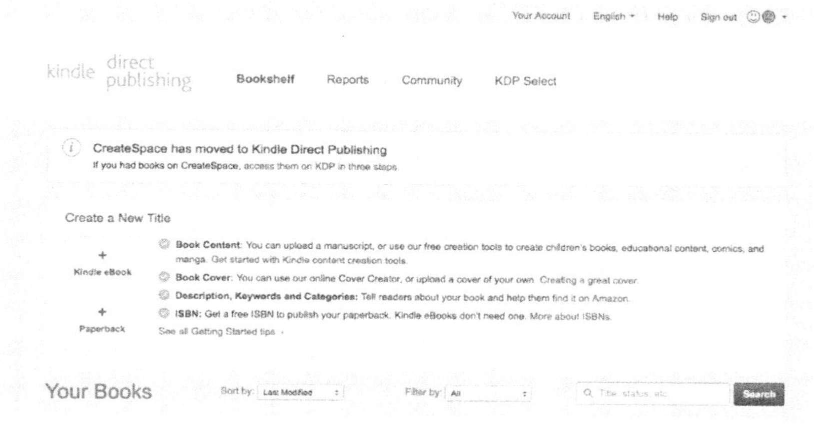

Figure 52: Bookshelf (KDP Home)

From here, you can start the process of uploading a book to KDP. I'll upload 'How to Write a Kindle Ebook' as an example.

Under the heading 'Create a New Title', I click on '+ Kindle eBook' to begin.

Now, I'm presented with a screen with three tabs from left to right: Kindle eBook Details, Kindle eBook Content, and Kindle eBook Pricing.

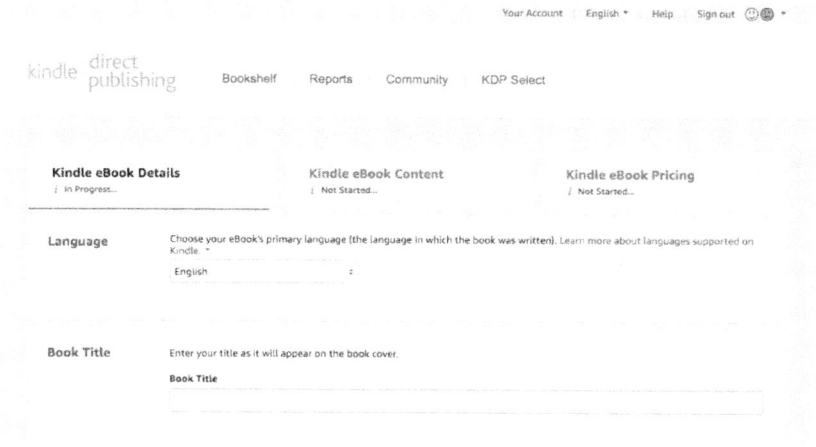

Figure 53: KDP add a Kindle eBook

I start with Kindle eBook details.

## Kindle eBook Details

### Language

Forty-four different languages are supported by Kindle, including Frisian, Northern Frisian and Eastern Frisian. The Western and Southern Frisians must be furious!

My book is in English. There's no option to choose between English (US), English (UK), or any other version of English.

### Book title

I add my book's title and (optionally) sub-title.

### Series, Edition Number

If your book is part of a series, add the series name and volume number. Also, if this is a new edition of an existing book, you can provide an edition number (e.g. '2' if you've made significant changes to the first edition).

### Author

I add my name as the author. If you've decided on a pen name, this is the place to use it (not in the Account Information, described above).

### Contributors

This is the area for adding the names of contributors you want to credit – co-author(s), editor, photographer, translator, illustrator, etc. If nobody needs crediting here, leave the boxes blank.

### Description

This is really important. It's what potential readers will see when they are browsing the Kindle Store, so – assuming they liked your cover and title - it will help sell your book.

You have a maximum of 4,000 characters. The description should set out in a clear and readable way exactly what readers can expect from your book. Why will it entertain them? Will they find it funny or gripping? What problem will it solve for them?

Make sure you get it right!

### Publishing rights

Most people will be publishing a work they've written themselves, so will choose 'I own the copyright and I hold the necessary publishing rights.'

The other, less likely, option is 'This is a public domain work'. An example could be re-publishing an old book (where the copyright has expired) as a Kindle ebook.

### Keywords

If you're used to doing keywords for websites, you might expect this to involve lots of repetition. Search Engine Optimisation for the web means choosing a few relevant words or phrases per web page, and using them in the page name, title, and description, as well as putting them in the page headings and text.

It's important to hammer away at the same words or phrases again and again and again. And again.

For ebooks it's different, apparently. KDP's advice is to choose keywords or short phrases that describe your book but *do not* repeat words in the title, description or (see below) category.

That makes it quite difficult! I used lots of relevant words and phrases in my title and description, and it's hard to find new ones for the keywords.

KDP's Help page for keywords, 'Make Your Book More Discoverable with Keywords'[31], suggests testing out the keywords you're considering by entering them in Amazon's search box. 'Think like a reader. Imagine how you would search if you were a customer'.

### Categories

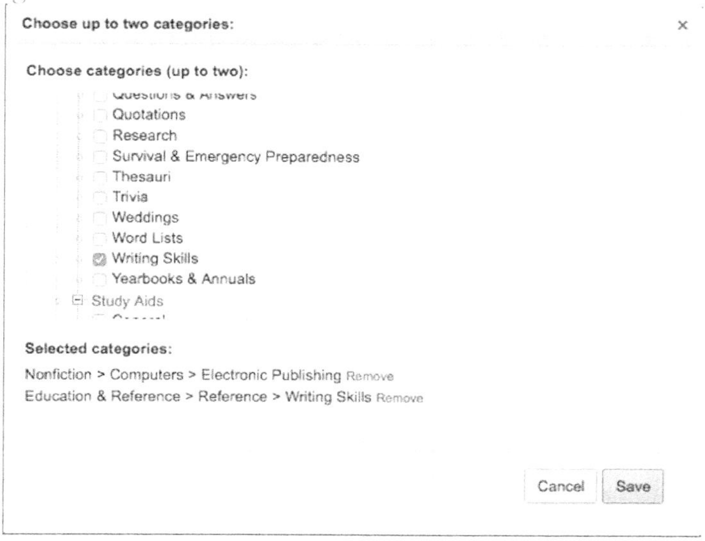

*Figure 54: my choice of KDP Categories*

You can select two 'browse categories'. Then if a customer browsing the Kindle Store refines their search to include your categories, your book should display in the search results.

To choose this book's categories, I expand the 'non-fiction' menu to see the options. I find 'Computers', and among the sub-options is 'Electronic

Publishing'. Bingo!

My other selection is Non-fiction > Reference > Writing Skills. Not bingo! But it's the best I can find.

The pop-up window showing my selections is in Figure 54 above.

### Age and Grade Range

Age and grade range are optional, and would apply to books for children or young adults. I assume that if you're thinking of writing a book, you already know how to read one – so I won't add any information here.

### Pre-order

There's a choice between:

- 'I am ready to release my book now', and
- 'Make my Kindle eBook available for Pre-order'

The tooltip explains that customers can pre-order a book up to a year before it's released, and it will automatically be delivered to their Kindles on release date.

The KDP Help for 'Kindle eBook Pre-Order'[32] adds that making a book available for pre-order means you can start promoting it before release.

You set a date, which is your deadline to submit the manuscript. You can put the date back once, for up to 30 days. After that if you don't upload the book to KDP, your pre-order will be cancelled, and you'll be barred from setting up pre-orders for a year.

What are the benefits of pre-order for an author? Lois Hoffman explains[33] that you can advertise your book pre-release, and line up reviews for launch day. 'Anticipation is a powerful driver. The lead-up to anything often generates as much excitement as the event itself.'

What are the benefits of pre-order for a reader? Sometimes there may be a price incentive, but more often readers pre-order books they know they definitely want. Lahni explains the motivation on a goodreads discussion forum[34].

'I pre-order the "gotta have it" sequels. Then I don't have to worry about them. They just show up! And since I gotta have it now I'll pay whatever the price is. Not many books fall into this category for me.'

Thus, there are good reasons why a well-established writer with a loyal following, like Hilary Mantel, would make a new book available for pre-order. She almost certainly has people who advertise her books in advance of release, to generate anticipation.

I'm not a well-established writer, this isn't a sequel, and I don't have any people! I therefore conclude that pre-order isn't for me, and choose 'I am ready to release my book now.'

If I don't want to move on to the next step yet, at the bottom of the page I can select 'Save as Draft'. Then, on my Bookshelf under the heading 'Your Books', my book appears as a draft.

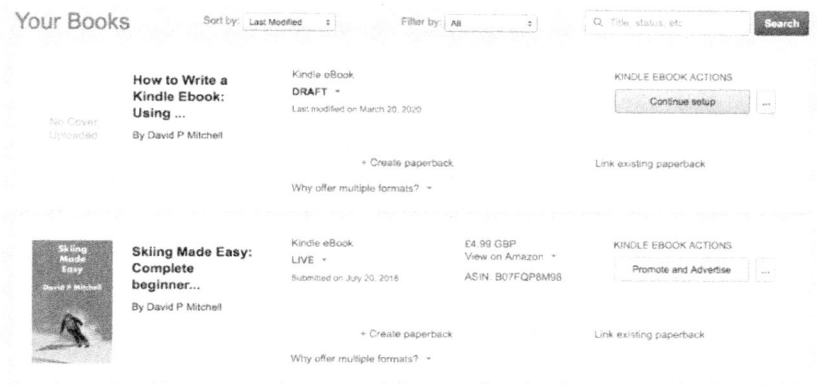

Figure 55: KDP Bookshelf shows my draft book

When I want to continue, I click 'Continue setup', and I'm taken back to the Kindle eBook Details page. This time, at the bottom of the page I'll click on 'Save and Continue' and I'm redirected to the Kindle eBook Content page.

Figure 56: KDP Kindle eBook Content page

There are four boxes to complete here – Manuscript, Kindle eBook Cover, Kindle eBook Preview, and Kindle eBook ISBN.

*Manuscript*

First, I'm asked to decide if I want to enable Digital Rights Management (DRM) on this ebook.

KDP's 'How is my Kindle eBook affected by DRM?' tooltip advice includes these words: 'DRM is intended to inhibit unauthorized distribution of the Kindle file of your book. Some authors want to encourage readers to share their work, and choose not to have DRM applied to their book.'

What decision should you make about DRM? Here is one viewpoint from an author, Charles O, contributing to the KDP Community forum[35].

'As an emerging indie author, my biggest issue is not profitability, it's obscurity. If I'm missing a few sales because someone who loves my book is sharing it, I count that as a net positive.'

'When I gain the following of a Jonathan Franzen or Jodi Picoult, I'll turn on DRM for my new releases. Until then, share away, my fans!'

Another author on the same forum thread, Suzanne, takes a different view.

'I always DRM. I also know what files are in my Kindle. It really isn't rocket science. Taking a file out of the Kindle is the easy part. Stripping the DRM out for the average person is not easy, but if it's not there, emailing the files around or uploading it to be downloaded to everyone in the world is super easy. Putting files on the readers is super easy. Stealing books, music, movies and other people's artwork is so casually accomplished that thieving is taken for granted with a shrug.'

I understand both points of view, but I find the first more convincing and more applicable to my situation than the second.

After making a decision about DRM, I'm invited to 'Upload eBook manuscript'.

I click on the Upload button, browse for the zip folder I created in Chapter 8, and upload it. A text box pops up with the message 'Save successful'. The Kindle eBook Content page then tells me 'Processing your file…' After a few seconds, the message 'Manuscript "how-to-write-a-kindle-ebook-march-2020.zip" uploaded successfully!' appears (Figure 57).

I take up the offer to view the '4 possible spelling errors': two are mistakes which I correct, and the other two are references to the 'kboard' forum. I change the spelling to 'KBoard', which makes it clear it's a brand name.

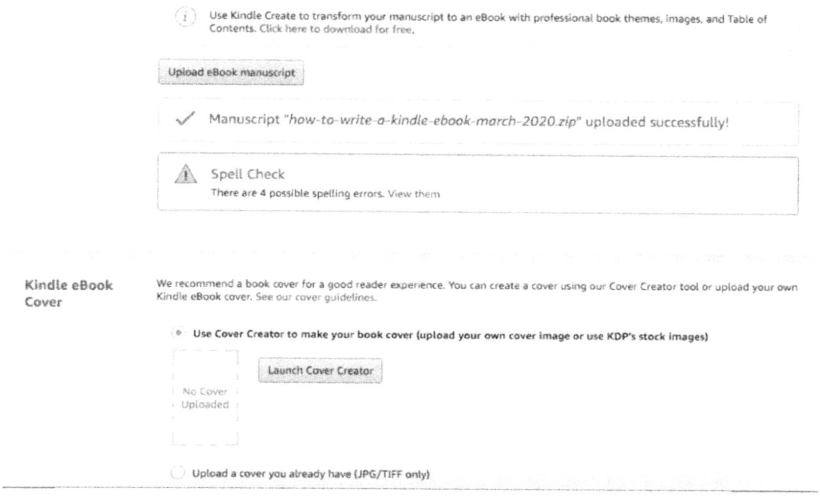

# HOW TO WRITE A KINDLE EBOOK

Figure 57: KDP manuscript uploaded successfully

## Cover

Now I can use the cover I prepared in Chapter 7. If you didn't create your own cover then, this is your opportunity to use KDP's Cover Creator tool.

I don't need Cover Creator, but I'll have a quick look at it anyway. This is the 'how to' page.

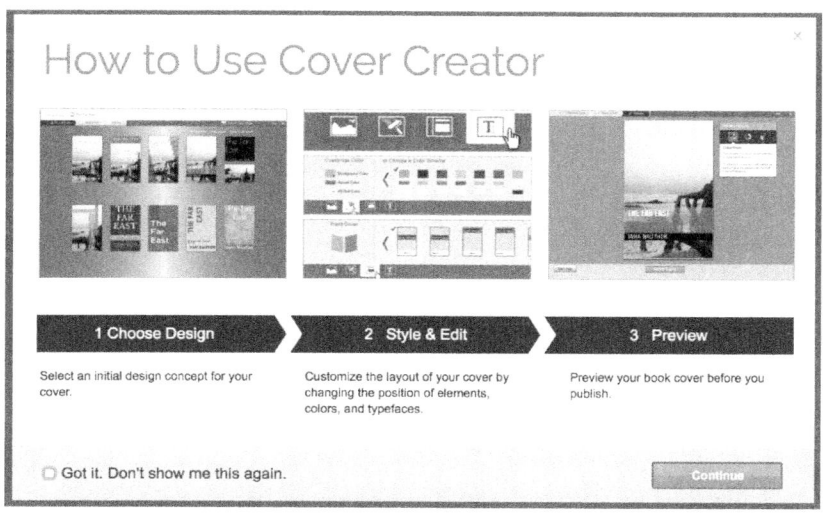

Figure 58: how to use Cover Creator

As you can see from the image above, there are three stages to the Cover Creator process: Design, Style & Edit, and Preview.

At the Design stage, Cover Creator offers me some image-based designs, and others ('non-image designs') that use patterns. All include my title, sub-title and author name.

Figure 59: choose Cover Creator design

I choose one of the non-image designs, and go on to Style & Edit. Here I can change the colours, layout and font.

Figure 60: Cover Creator Style & Edit

I then preview that cover, and if I'm happy with it, Save and Submit.

Figure 61: preview of Cover Creator cover

I wasn't expecting the Cover Creator process to be so easy and quick. You could use it to create a professional-looking cover in two minutes flat. Whoever developed that tool did a great job.

Your cover might lack a distinctive personal style, but if you just want to get your book out and on sale quickly, Cover Creator is a good choice. If you have more time later, you can always re-do the cover.

I'm going to stick with the cover I made in Chapter Seven, and select 'upload a cover you already have (JPG/TIFF only)'. It uploads in a few seconds.

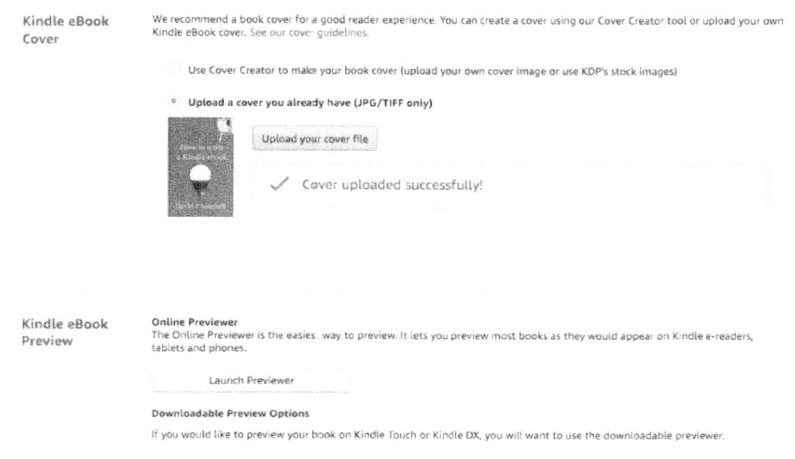

Figure 62: cover uploaded successfully

After uploading the cover I can go to the next step, previewing the book.

### Preview

You can preview your book online or using a download method.

If you choose to preview online, KDP uses your web browser to show you how it will look to readers. There are options at the top of the previewer, so you can change font size, and switch between simulated tablet, phone, or Kindle E-reader, as well as landscape or portrait mode.

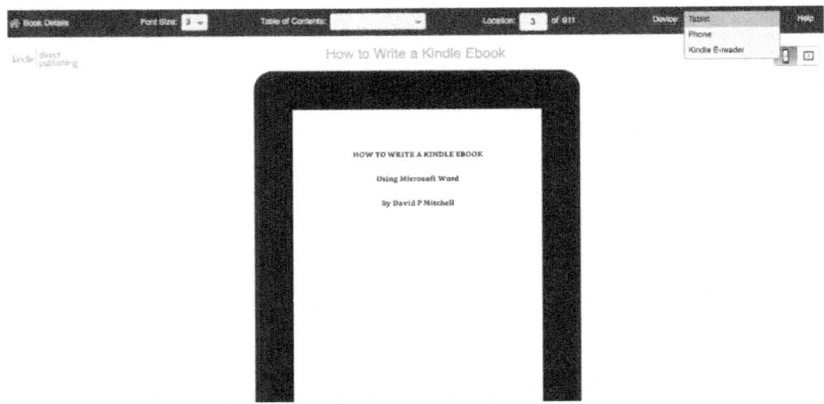

Figure 63: using the online Preview tool

It's worth taking your time at this stage, and checking right the way through your work.

I'd suggest your checks could include the following:

- that the links in the Table of Contents work
- that the links to the endnotes work, as well as the links from the endnotes back to the text
- that the formatting is as you expected
- click on any links to web pages to make sure they work
- make sure your images are centre-aligned and have a caption

You can always come back here later and use the Online Previewer tool, even after your book is published.

As well as the Online Previewer, there are Downloadable Preview Options.

### Preview on your computer

If you want to preview your book on your computer, you have to download and install the Previewer app, then choose between an HTML and a MOBI version of your book. (I believe the HTML version is similar to KDP's newer KF8 file format, and MOBI is very close to the older AZW format[36]).

When I download my book, the file goes to my computer's Downloads directory, and Kindle Previewer opens it.

### Preview on your Kindle device

To download and preview on a Kindle Touch or Kindle DX, download the HTML or MOBI file, then send it to your send-to-Kindle email address, as explained on Amazon's Send to Kindle by Email page[37].

Whichever preview option you choose, you can continue with the KDP upload process, and preview your book at your leisure.

### ISBN

The final part of the Content page is optional. You can enter an International Standard Book Number (ISBN) here, if you have one or if you go and buy one on the web.

You don't need an ISBN for an ebook. Amazon will allocate an Amazon Standard Identification Number (ASIN) to your ebook, and if you turn the book into a paperback, KDP will provide you with an ISBN for the paperback for free.

I'm going to leave the ISBN section blank. I can now Save and Continue to the third and final step, pricing.

## Kindle eBook Pricing

There are five sections to complete – KDP Select, Territories, Royalty and Pricing, Book Lending, and Terms and Conditions.

### KDP Select

When I published Skiing Made Easy, it was exclusive to KDP (in that there were no other versions, on iBooks, Google Play etc.), but I didn't enter it in the KDP Select programme.

That was partly because I was confused by all the brand names and buzzwords related to KDP Select, and I wasn't sure what was involved. I've now looked into it thoroughly, and I know exactly what's going on!

If your book is exclusive to KDP, you have the option to enrol in KDP Select.

Books enrolled in KDP Select can be read by customers who pay a monthly subscription for Kindle Unlimited. KDP sets aside a fund to pay Royalties to authors of books in KDP Select, and payments are made on the basis of the number of pages actually read by Kindle Unlimited subscribers.

This is an opportunity to make extra money. In general, if your book is exclusive to KDP it may as well be in KDP Select.

An exception would be if you think Kindle Unlimited subscribers will buy your book separately, if it's not included in their subscription. In that case, you should keep it out of KDP Select, because book sales will usually be worth more than the KDP Select 'per page read' fees.

Being in KDP Select also gives you more flexibility to promote your book, with special prices or free promotions for limited periods. When you've just published your book, this enables you to give the book away to reviewers, and get a free copy for your own Kindle library.

If you're not sure what to do about KDP Select, I suggest enrolling for the initial period of 90 days to take advantage of the promotional tools. If you then decide it's not for you, or you want to sell your book on other platforms, disable auto-renew.

For more of the details and intricacies of KDP Select, see my Appendix on the subject (p. 80).

(Who doesn't like an Appendix? It gives a book class - I hope! My Appendix definitely isn't as good as Appendix D of Mark Twain's classic, A Tramp Abroad, but it does tell you more about KDP Select than Twain's addendum[38].)

### Territories

Here, you're asked to select the territories for which you hold distribution rights.

Kindle's Help page says, 'If your book is original content and you've never published it before, you most likely have worldwide rights.'

That will apply to most people reading this book; if so, select 'All territories (worldwide rights)'.

### Royalty and pricing

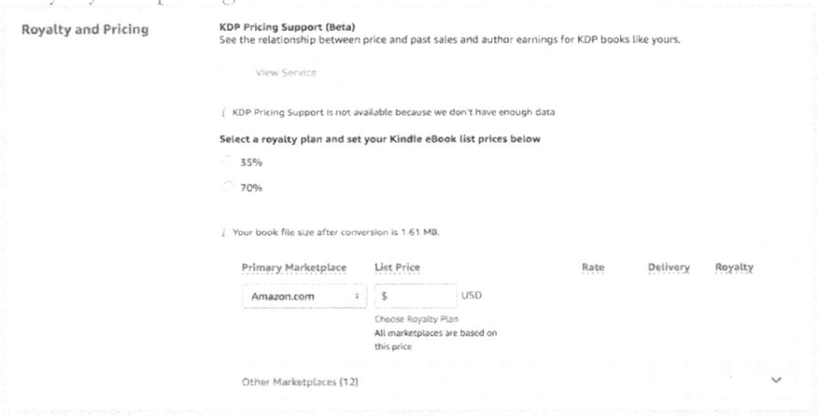

Figure 64: KDP Royalty and Pricing box

There are big decisions to be made here, not least the price you're going to charge.

If your book took you many weeks or months to write, you've probably been thinking about the price for some time, and this won't be a spur-of-the-moment decision.

The Royalty and Pricing box is shown in Figure 64 above.

I would like to use the KDP Pricing Support service to see what price they recommend, but in my case it isn't available.

The next decision to make is between 35% and 70% Royalties. Of course you should choose 70% Royalties if you can, but note:

- Your list price must be between $2.99 and $9.99, or equivalent for other territories (e.g. between £1.49 and £9.99 in the UK)
- You'll only get 35% in Brazil, Japan, Mexico and India, unless you're enrolled in KDP Select
- If your book is public domain content not original content, you're not eligible for 70%
- As discussed in Chapter 5, Images, if you choose 70% Royalties, Delivery Costs apply[39]; for a book with lots of images and a large file size, it may be more profitable to opt for 35% and no Delivery Costs

I choose Amazon.com as my Primary Marketplace for this book, on the basis that my target market is English-speaking people who want to write ebooks, and there are more such people in America than anywhere else.

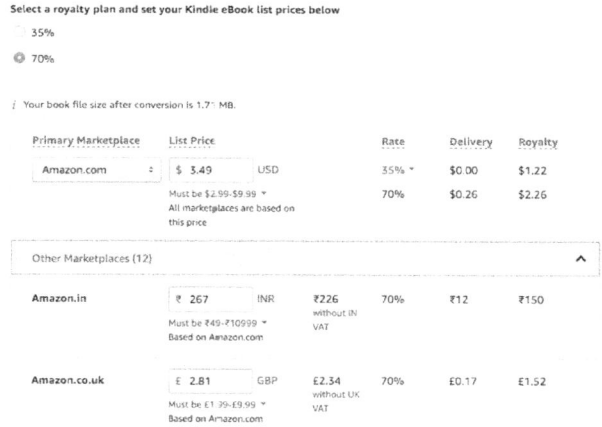

Figure 65: Royalties and Delivery Costs

I decide on a list price of $3.49, which is about the cost of a cup of coffee. I hope this book is worth at least as much as a Cinnamon Dolce Latte.

When I click on Other Marketplaces, KDP has generated prices in other countries' currencies, equivalent to $3.49 (see Figure 65 above).

I can adjust the prices in other marketplaces if I want them to be the sort of figures people expect to see (ending in .49 or .99).

KDP says my converted book is 1.71MB. The Delivery Cost is $0.15 per MB, which reduces my Royalty by $0.26. The Royalty per sale, $2.26, is still much better than it would be at the 35% rate - $1.22.

### Book Lending

A reader who has bought your book may lend it once to a friend or family member, for 14 days. As I've chosen 70% Royalties, I can't opt out of this; if I'd picked 35%, I could opt out.

### Terms and conditions

This box tells you:

- By clicking on 'Publish Your Kindle eBook', you're confirming that you have the rights to upload and distribute the book, and you're in compliance with the KDP Terms and Conditions
- It can take up to 72 hours for your book to become available to buy on Amazon

If you're ready, you can click 'Publish Your Kindle eBook'. You'll receive Congratulations in a pop-up box.

Figure 66: Congratulations! after submitting ebook

On your KDP Bookshelf, the status of your ebook becomes 'IN REVIEW' then changes to 'PUBLISHING'. It is reviewed by KDP within 72h (but often sooner), and you'll receive email notification when it's live and on sale on Amazon.

# 10 MAKING CHANGES AFTER PUBLICATION

One of the advantages of e-publishing is that small revisions are no big deal. You can make changes to your content or cover, and re-publish in a few clicks.

KDP say that if you make major changes, you should publish the revised version as a new book. This would involve adding a new ebook to your Bookshelf, and making sure to give it a new edition number on the Kindle eBook Details page. As the new ebook would have no reviews or sales ranking, this is not likely to be an attractive option for most authors.

To make minor changes, begin on your KDP Bookshelf. To the right of your book(s) is the heading 'KINDLE EBOOK ACTIONS'. Under that is a big button with a suggested action, and next to it is a smaller button with three dots on it (an ellipsis). Hover over the ellipsis, and more action options display.

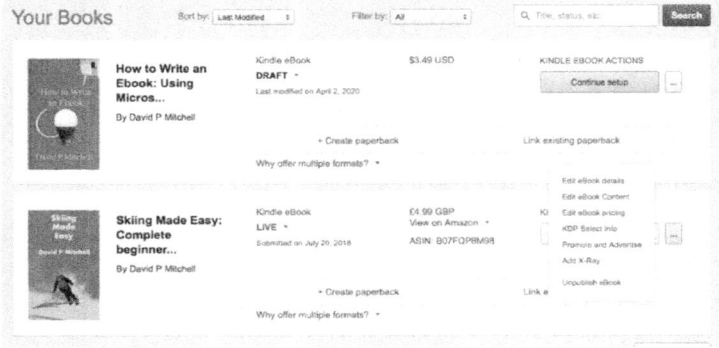

Figure 67: Kindle ebook actions

The first three options should be familiar from Chapter 9. They are Edit eBook Details, Edit eBook Content, and Edit eBook Pricing, and they take you back to the details, content and pricing pages you completed when uploading your ebook.

### Edit eBook details

If you choose to 'Edit eBook Details', you'll land on the Kindle eBook Details page.

You can change your book details, but note these points from KDP's Update Your Book Details Help page[40]:

- If you change the title and/or sub-title, remember to change it on your book cover and on the title page of your manuscript too
- If you make significant changes to your book, it is considered a new edition and should be published as a new book
- To save changes on the Kindle eBook Details page, you have to go through the content and pricing pages as well. Click Save and Continue at the bottom of the Kindle eBook Details page, Save and Continue at the bottom of the Kindle eBook Content page, and Publish Your Kindle eBook at the bottom of the Kindle eBook Pricing page
- KDP will review your changes and it can take up to 48h for them to go live[41]
- While your changes are being reviewed, the KINDLE EBOOK ACTIONS menu will be disabled, so you won't be able to do anything else until they are approved; this applies to changes to content, cover and pricing too

### Edit eBook Content

If you choose to 'Edit eBook Content', this will take you to the Kindle eBook Content page. Here, you can upload a revised version of your book and/or a new cover.

#### Changes to your content

Make the changes to your Word file, then convert it to HTML and create a zip file (as described in Chapter 8).

Then you can simply click on 'Upload eBook manuscript', find the zip file, and upload it (as described in Chapter 9). Preview your changes online or via download (see Chapter 9).

Note these points from KDP's Update Your Manuscript Help page[42]:

- Remember to edit your Kindle eBook details to match the revised

content, if necessary
- If you make significant changes, your book is considered to be a new edition and should be published as a new book
- Updates should be live within 48h; you'll receive email confirmation when this happens

### Receiving minor changes

In theory, Amazon customers can choose to receive Automatic Book Updates, in which case they should get the minor changes you've made[43].

To receive Automatic Book Updates, when signed in to Amazon select Your Account > Manage Your Content and Devices > Preferences tab > Automatic Book Updates, and set it to ON.

### Notifying customers of major changes

Authors used to be able to ask KDP to send emails to people who had bought the book, notifying them of major changes. Those customers could go to their Manage Your Kindle page on Amazon and get the update.

That procedure is described in Building Your Book for Kindle, but unfortunately the information is out of date.

Now KDP's Send Updated eBook Content to Customers Help page[44] says, essentially, that you can't. Not if you've edited the content, added or deleted chapters or images, or even changed the entire plot. The reason given is that updates can erase highlights or notes made by readers.

When you make major changes, you have to publish a new version of your book, but customers who had already bought it keep the old version.

The only circumstance where KDP will notify customers about changes is when you've corrected 'serious quality issues', also described as 'destructive or critical errors'. If you accidentally omitted the last ten pages of a whodunit – the part where readers find out that it was Professor Plum in the Library with the Candlestick – that should count.

If you did leave out the last ten pages from the file you uploaded, or need to contact KDP for any other reason, click on 'Contact Us'. It's in the footer menu of all KDP pages.

### Changes to your cover

The Kindle eBook Content page is also where you uploaded your cover. If you want to change it, just upload a new one.

As during the original upload process, you can choose to use Cover Creator or upload a new cover you've made yourself (in JPEG or TIFF format).

KDP's Update Your Cover Help page[45] asks you to make sure that the information on your updated cover matches that in your Kindle eBook Details on KDP, and on the title page of your book.

To save the updated content and/or cover, click Save and Continue at the bottom of the Kindle eBook Content page, and Publish Your Kindle eBook at the bottom of the next (pricing) page.

It can take 72h for your updated cover to go live in the Kindle store.

## Edit eBook Pricing

If you've changed your mind about the price, you can alter it on the Kindle eBook Pricing page.

Remember that if you want 70% Royalties, your price must be in the range $2.99-$9.99.

# 11 PROMOTING YOUR BOOK

Joining KDP Select gives you two ways of promoting your book – Kindle Countdown Deals and Free Book Promotions. Whether you're in KDP Select or not, you can run an Ad Campaign. There are other ways of promoting your book too.

## Kindle Countdown Deals

I'm going to set up a Kindle Countdown Deal for Skiing Made Easy.

From my Bookshelf, I select 'Promote and Advertise'. (In this case, it's the main option under KINDLE EBOOK ACTIONS; otherwise I could hover over the ellipsis and select it).

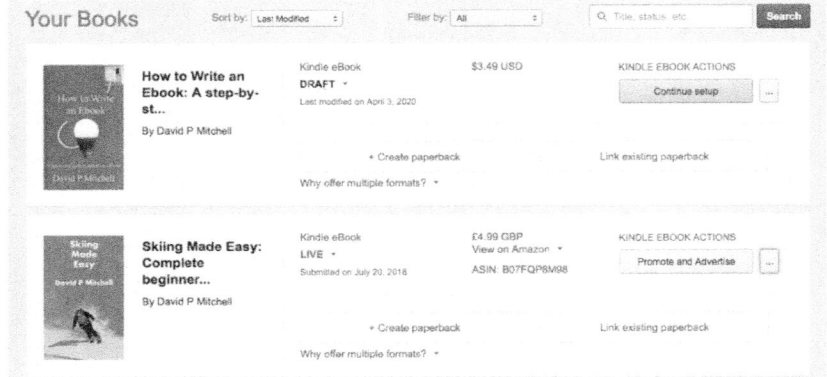

Figure 68: Bookshelf, with Promote and Advertise option

I land on the Promotions page for Skiing Made Easy.

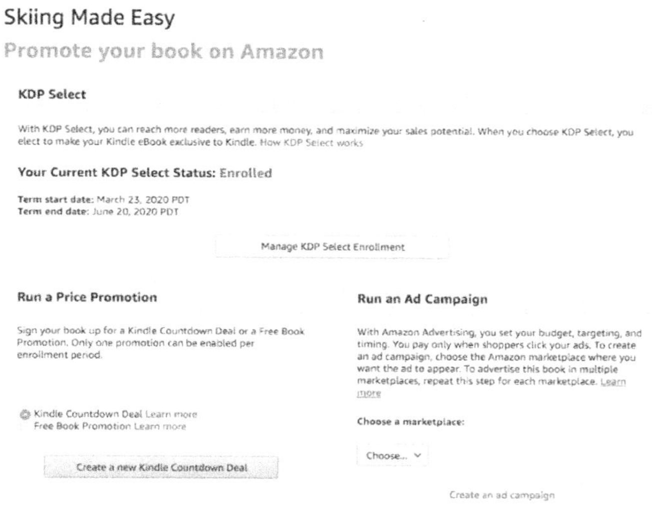


Figure 69: KDP Promotions page for Skiing Made Easy

Under 'Run a Price Promotion', I select Kindle Countdown Deal, and click on the button to create one.

That takes me to a page headed 'Create a new Kindle Countdown Deal'. I have three sections to complete: select marketplace, promotion will start and end, and price increments.

## Select marketplace

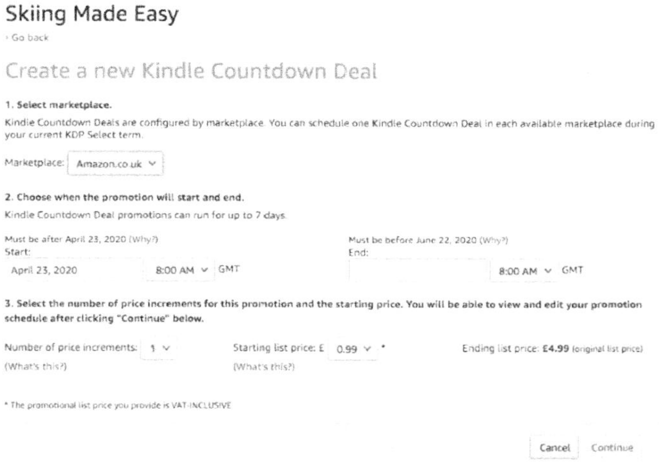


Figure 70: create a new Kindle Countdown Deal

Kindle Countdown Deals can be set up on Amazon.com and Amazon.co.uk. You can run promotions on both at the same time, but you set them up separately. I'll set up a promotion on Amazon.co.uk.

## Promotion start and end

I have to decide on a promotion start and end date.

Sales of Skiing Made Easy are seasonal anyway, but at the time of writing they are non-existent because ski resorts around the world are closed due to Coronavirus. As a result, the promotion dates I choose are academic.

The Countdown can't start before 23rd April 2020 (30 days after I enrolled my book in KDP Select) and it must end before 22nd June (when there are 14 days left on my KDP Select enrolment). Those rules are set out on the Kindle Countdown Deal Help page[46].

It can run for between 1 hour and 7 days. I decide to run it for 7 days from 23rd to 30th April 2020.

## Price increments

I'm offered up to four price points before returning to the original list price (£4.99). I'll use two in this example.

I'm asked to specify a 'starting list price', and the options are:

- £0.99
- £1.99, or
- £2.99

I choose £2.99. This is the completed form.

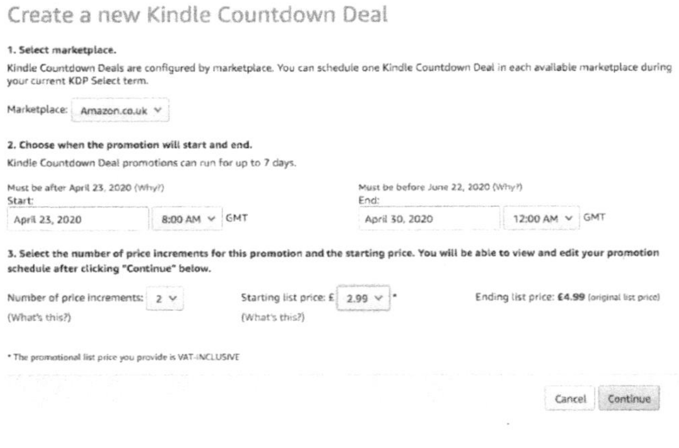

Create a new Kindle Countdown Deal

**1. Select marketplace.**

Kindle Countdown Deals are configured by marketplace. You can schedule one Kindle Countdown Deal in each available marketplace during your current KDP Select term.

Marketplace: Amazon.co.uk

**2. Choose when the promotion will start and end.**

Kindle Countdown Deal promotions can run for up to 7 days.

Must be after April 23, 2020 (Why?)
Start: April 23, 2020 8:00 AM GMT

Must be before June 22, 2020 (Why?)
End: April 30, 2020 12:00 AM GMT

**3. Select the number of price increments for this promotion and the starting price. You will be able to view and edit your promotion schedule after clicking "Continue" below.**

Number of price increments: 2 (What's this?)

Starting list price: £ 2.99 * (What's this?)

Ending list price: **£4.99** (original list price)

* The promotional list price you provide is VAT-INCLUSIVE

Cancel Continue

Figure 71: Kindle Countdown Deal form completed

When I click Continue, KDP calculates a promotion schedule, with two promotional prices as I requested, and the promotion period split evenly between them.

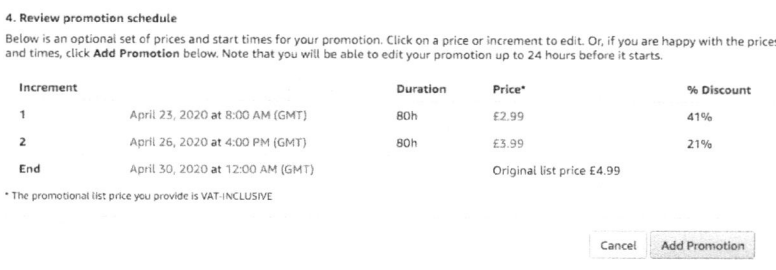

Figure 72: Kindle Countdown Deal promotion schedule

If I want to change a date or a price, I just click on it; in this case, the suggested promotion schedule will be fine, so I click 'Add Promotion'.

I receive a 'success' message, and I'm returned to the Promotions page.

## After setting up a Kindle Countdown Deal

After setting up a Kindle Countdown Deal:

- from my Bookshelf, under KINDLE EBOOK ACTIONS, I can click on Promote and Advertise to reach the Promotions page
- the details of the Kindle Countdown Deal I've set up are at the bottom of the Promotions page

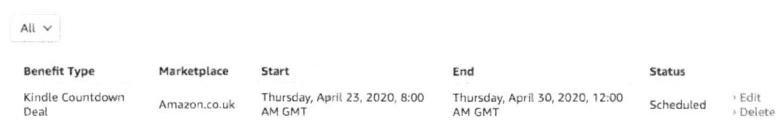

Figure 73: Kindle Countdown Deal details

- I can edit or delete it up to 24h before it begins
- Even if the discounted price is below the usual minimum to be eligible for 70% Royalties, I still receive 70%, but of the discounted price
- Having set up a Kindle Countdown Deal, I can't run a Free Book Promotion for Skiing Made Easy in the same 90 day period that it's entered in KDP Select; it's one or the other, not both

## Sales as a result of a Kindle Countdown Deal

Back in 2014, Alison Thompson set up a Kindle Countdown Deal for her book 'The Boy from Hell: Life with a Child with ADHD'[47].

She found that she sold a lot more books at the lower price during the Deal; but once it was over, sales were 'back to normal' – there didn't seem to be any enduring boost as a result of the extra exposure.

## Free Book Promotions

To set up a Free Book Promotion, go to the Promotions page, as I described for Kindle Countdown Deals. Under the heading 'Run a Promotion', toggle the radio button to 'Free Book Promotion', and click 'Create a new Free Book Promotion'.

Then you simply set a start and end date for your Free Book Promotion, and click Save Changes.

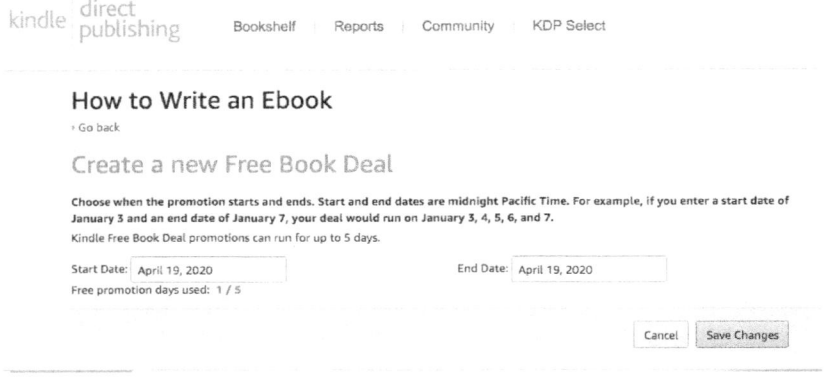

Figure 74: Free Book Promotion scheduled

You'll get a 'success' message, and the Free Book Promotion will show at the bottom of your book's Promotions page. As with Kindle Countdown Deals, you have the option to Edit or Delete.

According to the Kindle Help page for Free Book Promotions[48], you can offer your book free for up to 5 days of a 90 day enrolment period in KDP Select. This can be five consecutive days, or you can do several Free Book Promotions of one or more days at a time. It applies to all Kindle marketplaces.

Although you don't earn any money by giving your book away, Free Book Promotions are a good way of getting more readers and reviews. Schedule a Free Book Promotion, then tell family and friends about it, as well as media contacts, bloggers or other potential reviewers.

## Ad Campaigns

If you're wiling to pay to promote your book, you can launch an Ad Campaign on Amazon. Yes, there are always more ways for them to make money out of you!

These are the main points:

- Go to Bookshelf > Promote and Advertise, and on the Promotions page you can create an Amazon Advertising account
- Choose a marketplace, then Create an Ad Campaign
- It's cost-per-click (CPC) advertising – you pay when a customer clicks on your ad; they're sent to your product details page and they may decide to buy your ebook
- You choose between two ad types: Sponsored Products, which appear on the Amazon website, and Lockscreen, that are shown on Kindle owners' devices
- You set a total budget, and a max CPC you're willing to pay for a particular keyword or phrase; your ad will be shown if it wins an auction against other advertisers

For more details, see the Advertising for KDP Books Help page[49].

## Other ways of promoting your book

More ways of promoting your book are suggested on KDP's Promote Your Book Help page[50]. The include:

- Author Central – create your own Author Page on KDP, rather like Facebook or Twitter for authors
- Use your own website and social media account(s) to promote your book
- If you're part of the Amazon Associates programme (or you join it), you can use an affiliate link from your website to your book, and earn an extra 4% on sales (see KDP's Merchandising Tips[51], tip 8)
- Get some Customer Reviews, because potential readers will rely on them. You can ask friends and family to review, as long as you don't demand a review or influence what's in it. Ask for a review on the last page of your book, as anyone who has got that far must think it's worth reading; KDP also generates a Before You Go… page after your last page, that asks for a review
- You can buy copies of your ebook to give away – see KDP's Buying and Gifting eBooks for Others Help page[52]. You'll get some of the money you spend back in Royalties, but Amazon get their percentage too, so it would probably make more sense to schedule a

Free Book Promotion and tell people about it

You can see whether your efforts to promote your book have been successful by looking at your Reports; Reports is the second tab on the KDP website, next to Bookshelf.

Finally, you could look for more ideas or ask a question in Community (the third tab on the KDP website). It's a forum for KDP authors, and you can use it to find answers on any KDP-related subject. A quick look turns up a thread for 'What Is The Most Effective Promotion You've Ever Done?'[53] The top-rated answer advised sending out free copies of the ebook to appropriate blogs and magazines.

## 12 LOOKING AHEAD

I hope you've found How to Write a Kindle Ebook useful.

I've been through what to write; set out how to format the front matter and the chapters of your book, and how to create endnotes and a Table of Contents; discussed images; suggested three ways of designing a cover; explained how to convert your Word file to HTML; described the upload process and the decisions you have to make in that process; dealt with changes after publication; and provided ideas for promoting your book.

There are more publishing options beyond the scope of this book. For example, you could create a paperback through KDP (like this one), and/or sell your ebook on other platforms such as iBooks or Google Play.

If you could take a moment to give this book a rating and review (even if it's just one line), I'd very much appreciate it.

It's never been easier for someone with an idea and a little determination to write and publish a book. I wish you the best of luck with your project, and I hope you find the process hugely enjoyable and rewarding.

# APPENDIX: KDP SELECT

The KDP Select programme is open to Kindle books which are exclusive to KDP – i.e. there's no other digital version, for example on iBooks or Google Play. Basic information about KDP Select is available on the fourth tab of the KDP website.

## Signing up to KDP Select

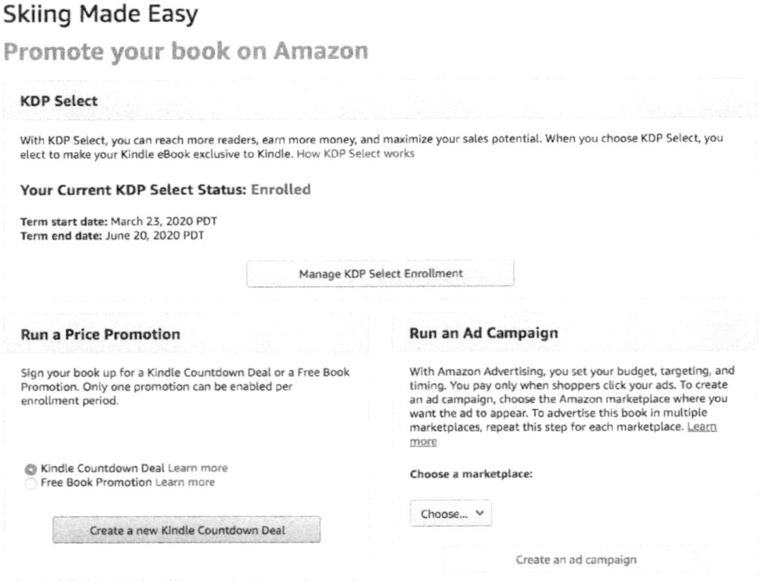

**Skiing Made Easy**

**Promote your book on Amazon**

**KDP Select**

With KDP Select, you can reach more readers, earn more money, and maximize your sales potential. When you choose KDP Select, you elect to make your Kindle eBook exclusive to Kindle. How KDP Select works

**Your Current KDP Select Status:** Enrolled

**Term start date:** March 23, 2020 PDT
**Term end date:** June 20, 2020 PDT

Manage KDP Select Enrollment

**Run a Price Promotion**

Sign your book up for a Kindle Countdown Deal or a Free Book Promotion. Only one promotion can be enabled per enrollment period.

○ Kindle Countdown Deal Learn more
○ Free Book Promotion Learn more

Create a new Kindle Countdown Deal

**Run an Ad Campaign**

With Amazon Advertising, you set your budget, targeting, and timing. You pay only when shoppers click your ads. To create an ad campaign, choose the Amazon marketplace where you want the ad to appear. To advertise this book in multiple marketplaces, repeat this step for each marketplace. Learn more

Choose a marketplace:

Choose... ⌄

Create an ad campaign

Figure 75: page displayed after enrolling in KDP Select

You can choose to sign up to KDP Select as you're uploading your book to KDP, on the Kindle eBook Pricing page.

If you decide to sign up at a later date, go to your Bookshelf page, find the book you want to enrol, and one of the available actions is to enrol in KDP Select. The page displayed after enrolling in KDP Select (the Promotions page) is shown in Figure 75 above.

Unless you change your mind and cancel within the first 3 days, your book will stay in KDP Select for 90 days. After that, participation in the programme will be auto-renewed for another 90 days. If you don't want to renew, go to your Bookshelf, and on the book's actions select 'Manage KDP Select Enrollment' then un-tick the auto-renew box.

### Benefits of KDP Select

There are several benefits to being in the KDP Select programme – opportunities to make extra Royalties, and more flexibility in promoting your book. I run through the details in the next few paragraphs.

### Kindle Unlimited

Customers who pay a monthly subscription to Kindle Unlimited (KU) can download your book when it's in KDP Select, and you're paid per page read.

Kindle books don't have a set number of pages, but KDP calculates pages according to a formula it calls Kindle Edition Normalized Page Count.

The money paid to authors comes from a fund set up by KDP, and called the KDP Select Global Fund.

### Kindle Owners' Lending Library

As well as being available to KU subscribers, when it's in KDP Select your book can be read by Amazon Prime customers in the US, UK, Germany, France and Japan. This is under a scheme called the Kindle Owners' Lending Library (KOLL), which allows Prime customers to choose one book a month at no extra cost.

### How much do you earn from KU and KOLL?

Reedsyblog[54] has a good article on KDP Select.

They looked at the KDP Select Global Fund in January 2019, and found that it was $24.7 million, with a pay out of $0.0044 per page read. As a result, the author of a 300-page book would be paid $1.32 every time it was read right through.

That's almost certainly less than the price of the book bought as a one-off. It's better than nothing, so if you think KU subscribers will limit themselves to books included in their subscriptions, you may as well join

KDP Select. If, on the other hand, you think they'll buy your book outside of KU if it's not included, it would be better not to join KDP Select.

(The KDP Select Global Fund in February 2020 is $27.2 million).

### Brazil, Japan, India and Mexico

Being in KDP Select means you earn 70% Royalties in these countries, where otherwise the rate would only be 35%.

### Kindle Countdown Deal

If you're in KDP Select, you can run a Kindle Countdown Deal. This means promoting your book by offering it at a reduced price for a limited period on Amazon.com and Amazon.co.uk.

Potential readers will be able to see the usual price, the reduced price and the time left to take advantage of the offer.

There are various limitations in the small print. For example, your promotion can only start once your book has been in KDP Select for 30 days. There are more details in Chapter 11 and on the Kindle Countdown Deal Help page.

### Free Book Promotion

If you're in KDP Select, you can run a Free Book Promotion for 5 days of the 90 that you're signed up to the programme. This is *instead of* (not as well as) a Kindle Countdown Deal. There are more details in Chapter 11 and on the Free Book Promotions Help page.

When you first publish your book, you might want to ask your family and friends to review it, and get a copy for your own Kindle library. This would be a good time to run a Free Book Promotion.

More generally, it could help achieve a wider readership and more reviews for your book.

# REFERENCES

1 Ebook sales are growing, but news reports sometimes suggest the contrary. Such reports are usually based on figures from the American Association of Publishers. Their data are collected from Association members, who are trade publishers (https://publishingwithlove.com/ebook-publishing-industry-market-analysis-kindle/), and they don't include self-published Kindle ebooks which make up a large share of the ebook market. Amazon doesn't make ebook sales information public, though, so it's not possible to quote exact sales figures (https://www.authormedia.com/228/).

2 The 2017 figures are in a PublishDrive blog (https://blog.publishdrive.com/amazon-ebook-market-share/), and the graphic reproduced there was originally created by authorearnings.com.

3 This refers to the Publishing With Love article mentioned in reference 1.

4 https://geoffaffleck.com/10-best-selling-non-fiction-book-topics/

5 https://www.makealivingwriting.com/excuse-earning-freelance-writer-now/

6 https://www.huffpost.com/entry/do-ebook-customers-prefer_b_1457011

7 https://mybookcave.com/authorpost/ebook-word-count-does-size-matter/

8 The Creative Penn https://www.thecreativepenn.com/how-to-self-publish-an-ebook/

9 https://howtowriteanebook.info/wp-content/uploads/2020/03/building-your-book-for-kindle.pdf

10 https://en.wikipedia.org/wiki/Pilcrow

11 https://en.wikipedia.org/wiki/Preface

12 https://www.dorrancepublishing.com/what-is-a-prologue/

13 https://www.kboards.com/index.php?topic=121845.0

14 There's an exception to the rule that all images in Kindles are JPEGs. Kindle Format 8 (.kf8), which is used for ebooks read on Kindle Fire devices, supports GIF, BMP, PNG and SVG images as well as JPEGs. That's according to KDP Help Image Guidelines – Reflowable here https://kdp.amazon.com/en_US/help/topic/G75V4YX5X8GRGXWV

15 There's no advice about image captions in Building Your Book for Kindle, but the KDP Help page for images (referenced in endnote 14) has suggestions for captions if you're writing or editing your book in HTML not Word. It suggests putting the caption below the image (!) and using a separate HTML 'div' for the caption – which probably means the image and caption are separable not inseparable, i.e. they might end up on different pages.

16 https://williamspaniel.com/2012/09/22/how-to-format-images-for-kindle/

17 https://lithub.com/a-brief-history-of-book-illustration/

18 https://www.parkwestgallery.com/what-are-illuminated-manuscripts-and-how-were-they-created/

19 Make More Money on Kindle by Reducing your .mobi file size
https://www.creativindie.com/make-more-money-on-kindle-by-reducing-your-mobi-file-size/

20 Derek Haines on Just Publishing Advice
https://justpublishingadvice.com/amazon-kdp-delivery-costs-can-eat-at-your-royalty/

21 John Doppler, 'Are You Losing Money on KDP Delivery Fees?' Alliance of Independent Authors Blog
https://selfpublishingadvice.org/are-you-losing-money-on-kdp-delivery-fees/

22 https://valthorensguide.co.uk/wp/skiing-made-easy-photo-gallery/

23 https://howtowriteanebook.info/image-gallery/

24 How to Format Picture Books for Kindle and ePub3, Fiction Notes/Darcy Pattison http://www.darcypattison.com/publishing/format-picture-books-kindle/

25 https://answers.microsoft.com/en-us/mac/forum/macoffice2011-macword/clickable-table-of-contents-in-word-for-mac/98804470-dc72-4037-a73a-036e3673c358

26 In Chapter XI of Twain's A Tramp Abroad, he describes taking Lessons in Art from the best German painters. 'Whatever I am in Art I owe to these men. I have something of the manner of each and all of them; but they all said that I had also a manner of my own, and that it was conspicuous. They said there was a marked individuality about my style, - insomuch that if I ever painted the commonest type of dog, I should be sure to throw a something into the aspect of that dog, which would keep him from being mistaken for the creation of any other artist. Secretly I wanted to believe all these kind sayings, but I could not; I was afraid that my masters' partiality for me, and pride in me, biased their judgment.'

27 https://www.geekwire.com/2019/new-survey-estimates-amazon-prime-membership-u-s-exceeds-100m/

28 https://www.theguardian.com/business/2019/mar/07/almost-90-of-uk-shoppers-use-amazon-research-reveals

29 https://kdp.amazon.com/en_US/help/topic/G200620010

30 https://kdp.amazon.com/en_US/help/topic/G200641050

31 https://kdp.amazon.com/en_US/help/topic/G201298500

32 https://kdp.amazon.com/en_US/help/topic/G201499380

33 Lois Hoffman article on Happy Self-Publisher, Should you Use Kindle Pre-order? http://happyselfpublisher.com/should-you-use-kindle-pre-order/

34 Goodreads discussion forum on the subject 'What is the point of pre-ordering a book?' https://www.goodreads.com/topic/show/466086-what-is-the-point-of-pre-ordering-a-book

35 https://www.kdpcommunity.com/s/question/0D5f400001lmqyoCAA/drmyes-or-no?language=en_US

36 Mobipocket was a French company, founded in 2000, that developed the MOBI (.mobi) file format. Amazon bought it in 2005, and used MOBI as the basis for its ebooks; the .azw format is almost identical to .mobi. Kindle Format 8 (.kf8) was introduced in 2011 for Kindle Fire devices. It 'supports a subset of HTML5 and CSS3 features' – in other words, it's very much like a modern web page. This information is from Wikipedia's Mobipocket page https://en.wikipedia.org/wiki/Mobipocket

37 https://www.amazon.com/gp/sendtokindle/email

38 Appendix D of A Tramp Abroad is titled The Awful German Language. It's a semi-fictional account of Twain's struggles to learn the German tongue, and it's a great piece of comic writing.

I could have picked out almost any paragraph and it would have been brilliant, but I've stumbled on this one, with his suggestions for improving the German language.

"In the first place, I would leave out the Dative Case. It confuses the plurals; and besides, nobody ever knows when he is in the Dative Case, except he discover it by accident,-and then he does not know when or where it was that he got into it, or how long he has been in it, or how he is ever going to get out of it again. The Dative Case is but an ornamental folly,-it is better to discard it."

39 See KDP's Digital Pricing Page for Delivery Costs
https://kdp.amazon.com/en_US/help/topic/G200634500

40 https://kdp.amazon.com/en_US/help/topic/G200736410

41 See the KDP Timelines Help page
https://kdp.amazon.com/en_US/help/topic/G202173620

42 https://kdp.amazon.com/en_US/help/topic/G202176900

43 Automatic Book Updates are suggested as the solution on KDP's Send Updated eBook Content to Customers Help page https://kdp.amazon.com/en_US/help/topic/G200966010. In practice, this doesn't work for me. I don't get any changes I make to my own ebook – the version in my Kindle Library stays the same.

One workaround is to go to the Home page of the Kindle app on the device where you read Kindle ebooks, and from the actions menu choose 'Remove from Device'. Then go to Amazon > Manage Your Content and Devices and re-download the (revised version of the) book to your device. This method is hit and miss, in my experience. Sometimes it works, sometimes not.

44 https://kdp.amazon.com/en_US/help/topic/G200966010

45 https://kdp.amazon.com/en_US/help/topic/G200965970

46 https://kdp.amazon.com/en_US/help/topic/G201293780

47 What Happened When I Ran a UK Kindle Countdown Deal on theprooffairy.com http://www.theprooffairy.com/publishing/uk-kindle-countdown-deal/

48 https://kdp.amazon.com/en_US/help/topic/G201298240

49 https://kdp.amazon.com/en_US/help/topic/G201499010

50 https://kdp.amazon.com/en_US/help/topic/G201723090

51 https://kdp.amazon.com/en_US/help/topic/G200673650

52 https://kdp.amazon.com/en_US/help/topic/G200652260

53 What Is The Most Effective Promotion You've Ever Done? is a thread on KDP Community started by John Coviello here https://www.kdpcommunity.com/s/question/0D52T000050oZJwSAM/what-is-the-most-effective-promotion-youve-ever-done?language=en_US. The Top Rated Answer is sending out free review copies to appropriate blogs and magazines.

54 https://blog.reedsy.com/kdp-select

# ABOUT THE AUTHOR

David P Mitchell is the author of Skiing Made Easy – Complete Beginner to Parallel Turns. It's a practical guide to learning to ski, based on many happy seasons of ski teaching in Val Thorens. Having enjoyed writing and publishing that ebook, he wanted to share what he had learned in the process – hence this book, How to Write a Kindle Ebook.

# ACCOMPANYING WEBSITE

I've set up a website to accompany this book,
https://howtowriteanebook.info.
All the images are reproduced there in an image gallery, as well as the references from the ebook. (There are rather more references in this paperback because I don't have the option to create hyperlinks, so the numbering of the references on the website doesn't match the numbering of the references here).
The website also has a blog with posts on interesting developments in e-publishing. Finally, if you wish you can sign up to the website to comment on blog posts and ask or answer questions on the forum.

Printed in Great Britain
by Amazon